DIVORCED...
NOW WHAT?

Much has been written about divorce as a topic to be found in the self-help section of your favorite bookstore. Often the theme is about self-preservation or some theme of victimization, tough it out, get yours, etc. And very seldom do you find the matter of divorce shared from the guy's perspective.

Lynn has dared to do just that and to be very vulnerable in sharing his journey through divorce. From being a successful businessman with three children, the big house, pool, etc., eighteen years of marriage, only to find himself living in a back bedroom of his widowed mother's house. He shares it all. The bitterness, resentment, embarrassment, fearfulness and the journey he never expected in all of his life.

He will tell you it's not all well, even now, it still hurts, some days it's still rough, but, how he knows that it can get better, and it can for you. This inspirational read is not a "how-to" divorce manual, but it is an honest sharing of the journey through divorce, including "now what."

Dr. Roy Stoddard, Ph.D.
Farmington, New Mexico

Dear Lynn,

Two things--, first I thought your book was excellent!

Really well done! It would be more than helpful to someone going through a divorce, or one who has already gone though one.

Second, it taught me what my son David went though, I had no idea … no wonder he would not let me come to be with him. It must have been terrible, for him and for you!!!

I am *so sorry,* I wouldn't want *anyone* to go through what you and David did.

With much love to you,
Shirley,
Loveland, Colorado (Mother of a divorced son)

Dear Lynn,

First of all, we have read every word of your manuscript from "Dad" to "Dump" and found them full of thought and insight. We have also pondered over some of our favorite D words and found ourselves deeply engaged in conversation as we reflected how this could be used by pastors with divorced men in their congregations today.

I am blessed that you gave us the privilege to be in your *test market* as you labored over your manuscript. Although we have never had to experience the heartache and long journey to wellness that recovering from a divorce entails, one thing we have learned from our pilgrimage with the Lord is that He never wastes anything! An excellent example of this is Joseph's declaration about God when he reassures his brothers after Jacob's death.

> "You intended to harm me, but God intended
> it for good to accomplish what is now being done,
> the saving of many lives. (Genesis 50:20)

You and we both know that God never promotes sinful behavior, but in His great goodness, He takes the worst that comes into our lives and uses it to accomplish good. You have turned an incredible hurt and headache into something that God will use to restore life to the many fellow-sufferers who will read this book.

Your honest sharing not only has ***"market value"*** to those seeking to live a life restored to usefulness after the dreaded "D" of divorce; but speaking for ourselves, your sharing of your own pilgrimage opens up a floodgate of understanding to those who have and will have loved ones, family or friends, who are dealing with the aftermath of their own failed marriages.

For us, we will now have a much greater compassion in listening, should we be given the opportunity to hear someone's own experience of hurting so deeply. We have not been impressed that you make any changes to what you have related; your personal insights are the result of allowing God's word and His Spirit's insight to teach you, and you have shown that you are a willing learner. Your honesty and personal insights are refreshing.

With love and best wishes for all your efforts in helping others come to a relationship with our Lord and Savior Jesus Christ,

John and Sara Preston,
Pastor Emmanuel Baptist Church,
retired

P.S. – I have always appreciated God's awesome sense of humor; and your sense of humor communicated throughout your writing is wonderful! Especially delightful to me was the page titled *"Divine Intervention"*.

Best Wishes, Lynn. You speak from the heart. You will help other divorcees by sharing your stories through your own reflections. In this way, others learn from you in an indirect way as opposed to being hit over the head with your message. Personalizing your stories in what YOU have learned provides insight for others to learn from you and take away connections for them. I guess your D words are meditations that have led you to insightful levels of growth and moving on. Congratulations!

Francis Vitali, Ph.D.
University of New Mexico, Farmington Campus

Divorce … Not a word that any of us want to even think about, much less have to apply to our personal lives! The trials and tribulations associated with all aspects of Divorce have the ability to either tear a man down to his core, or act as a catalyst to rebuild his life in a wildly constructive and positive way! This , " Man to Man Guide to Getting

Through Divorce", not only helped me gain a deep understanding for the challenges involved but also gain the strength and desire to be the man I was destined to be.

Come on Guys, it's a quick easy read that can help you learn, understand, cope and discover a part of yourself that will help you move forward with confidence and enthusiasm.

Dr. Ryan T. Rowse DC, APC

John "JB" Butigan, CEO of Peak Seminars, says, "Lynn Blackwood has taken a word that most people don't like to discuss, "Divorce", and made it appealing to address for every man facing the myriad of challenges brought by this life-altering experience. "Divorced… now what?" gives the reader a fresh perspective to successfully build a fulfilled life by providing clarity and positive solutions that has never been given to those of us looking for answers.

John "JB" *has conducted over 9,000 meetings to over 3,000 different companies and organizations. He has personally trained over 450,000 people over the last 20 years, spanning all areas of personal and professional success. Peak has inspired millions of people to reach the pinnacle of success by attending their high-impact seminars, across North America.*

Client list includes, FEDEX, Nordstrom, Apple, Ritz Carlton, Disney, NFL, PGA Tour, NASCAR, The Bill and Melinda Gates Foundation and Harley Davidson.

About the Author

Lynn A. Blackwood earned a BBA from New Mexico State University. His working career in ministry includes serving with Campus Crusade for Christ/CRU at both the University of Minnesota and the University of Northern Colorado, working as a youth pastor at Emmanuel Baptist Church, and missionary stints in Mexico, the Philippines, and China. Lynn is also a board member with the National Day of Care. This international ministry features, "Houses of Hope", which sends teams to Nairobi, Kenya, to build homes for orphaned children. Lynn also studied at the International School of Theology. Lynn worked as a firefighter, and currently holds a management position with a regional Foodservice company where he has been recognized for his significant contribution. Blackwood is the author of *C if you Agree.* He has three grown children and currently lives in his home state of New Mexico.

Visit him on line at www.lynnblackwood.com.

DIVORCED... NOW WHAT?

A Practical, Man-to-Man Guide to Getting through Divorce

Solutions for Divorced Men to Move beyond Pain and Anger and Rebuild a Joyous, Fulfilling Life

LYNN A. BLACKWOOD

CrossBooks™
A Division of LifeWay
1663 Liberty Drive
Bloomington, IN 47403
www.crossbooks.com
Phone: 1-866-879-0502

First published by CrossBooks 1/21/2013

ISBN: 978-1-4627-2479-6 (sc)
ISBN: 978-1-4627-2478-9 (hc)
ISBN: 978-1-4627-2480-2 (e)

Library of Congress Control Number: 2013901051

Definitions taken from Webster's New World Dictionary

Printed in the United States of America

CONTENTS

Part 2 - Post-Divorce, Forgiveness and Hope Are Your Keys for Your New Life

Acknowledgments

As a man who's been divorced for seven years, I know that divorce is not an easy road. While I wrote this book, I was blessed to have some fellow divorced people—six men and one woman—reading my work and pushing back with their thoughts and experiences. I wish to thank them all: Randy Akins, Randy Dean, Judge Bill Liese, Jon Burton, John "JB" Butigan, Steve Foster, and Lisa Martin.

Also a special acknowledgment to Reverend John and Sara Preston. What they mean to me: priceless!

Special acknowledgments also go to my close friend and neighbor Dr. Francis Vitali, Ph.D., and to Ana Thompson, a VIP in my life. Gale, thank you for your investment in this project.

I also would not have made it through this very dark time without the help of my mother, Mary Blackwood. She immediately opened up her home to me when I had nowhere to go. It took me almost two years to get back on my feet, and she was so kind and respectful while her son was in a free fall for part of that stay. It's not easy to move back in with your mother at forty-seven, but we made it work and I am so grateful for her love.

My children, Zach, Kamy, & KK, all shuttled away to another man's house and forced to deal with a divorce at such a young age. It was so difficult to adjust to saying goodnight by texting on a cell phone, when before we always shared a nightly hug, a kiss and a prayer. Now they are young men and women and doing incredibly well, and I am so proud of them. We are all moving forward and looking for God's favor and leaving blame for others to discuss. I am so proud to be their dad and it's my privilege to help launch them into the destiny that God has for them, and to be about my own as well.

My two sisters, Leah Ann Manning and Lisa Martin—thank you for never leaving my side and understanding my plight. Your positive words of encouragement fueled my comeback and healing. I am so blessed to have you both as sisters in Christ and in this life—two times blessed!

Sarah Andrews – ***Sundragon Editing***, this lady is phenomenal, although we have never met face to face, she gets me like few people that I know. Our correspondence has been only through email and phone conversations, yet she can take my thoughts and help me make sense with them and get them on paper for you to read and enjoy. Thank you Sarah, you are the best!

editor@sundragonediting.com
http://www.sundragonediting.com/

Greg Morgan – ***Greg M. Photography***, again another woman in my life that has believed in this project and in me. Her and her husband, Dr. John Morgan (our pastor) has hung in there and supported me and my children during the best and darkest days of the past 7 years. She has an incredible gift in capturing on film just what you are looking for. I highly recommend her!

www.gregmphotography.com

Prologue

This book is not a tell-all, where I set out to expose my ex-wife and air out our dirty laundry. In fact, at this point in our relationship we are doing quite well as friends and parents of our three wonderful children.

As I went through the jagged teeth of divorce and then heard stories of other men's experiences, I was moved to write and try to help men who would come after me and find themselves dealing with this issue. Some of the stories you will read in this book are indeed mine, while others are from conversations with the men I spoke to as I was researching my content. This book contains no malice or even the hint of trying to bring harm to my marriage partner of eighteen years. These are just my thoughts of the hurt, the trials and the recovery of one divorced man.

To those men who are picking up this book for the first time, thank you! I hope that you find healing and a healthy desire to go on living your life in a positive manner. I also believe that the scriptures and encouragement contained within the covers of this book can prove to be the difference in your recovery.

Divorce is not fun; in fact it's one of the most hellish things I can think of, especially when children are involved. Take your time with this book and let the pages sink deep in your soul as you come to grips with your divorce and your new path. My goal with this book is to help as many men as I can, so after you're done with it, pass it on if you meet up with another man going through a divorce.

I am truly sorry for your pain, and I can say from my personal experience that life does get better and your heart will stop hurting with time. During your divorce, time will be your worst nightmare and then it will turn around and be your best friend. Life does get better and the hurt does subside, but you must do the hard work of recovery for yourself and your children. Do it for those you love and do it for yourself—and if you have a desire to one day marry again, do it for her. All of these people deserve a recovered man who won't go backwards for pity's sake, but who will live in the present with his eyes on the glorious future that God can provide. Blessings to you as you read this effort of mine!

Lynn Blackwood

FOREWORD

It was late spring when Mr. Clark came to my office for an intake interview. According to the phone conversation, he wanted to talk about his ex-wife and some trouble he was having. He was a large man, wearing a suit and tie as he walked through the door with his intake form in hand. He handed it to me.

We sat a couple of minutes doing small talk to get acquainted, and I learned that he was an investment broker, with real estate holdings—apartment rentals and commercial units—throughout Texas. In fact, he said with a chuckle that he didn't know how much he had or what he was worth. The chuckle was masking arrogance, pride and selfishness.

I pressed to the issue of why he came. He reported having been married for fifteen years, but was now divorced and was having problems with his ex-wife. He went on to say that he hadn't seen or heard from her for quite a while; didn't know where she was. Anger became a clear undertone in his voice as he told me more of his story.

"She just keeps messin' with my thoughts. I can't get her off my mind. She really screwed me over, taking tens of thousands of dollars!" Now his face was becoming red.

"May I ask a question, Mr. Clark?" I asked in monotone as I purposely interrupted his tirade.

"What?!" He took on a puzzled look. I paused.

"Actually, two questions, sir. How long have you been divorced and what's in it for you to let her live rent free in your head?"

He quickly turned red, again, as he sat in silence. His presence changed. "Ten years and I don't know." Sadness and puzzlement had taken over the anger.

"Good, you have a homework assignment. When you come back, I expect you to have the answer to the question. Call me if you have questions. Let's schedule for two weeks."

The good news is Lynn has moved forward without the collected baggage Mr. Clark had accumulated. In this read he makes himself vulnerable through his journey to help you.

Here Lynn shares his insights, disappointments, and seemingly small wins in the battle to move forward. This work of Lynn's is not pop psych or a "how-to for self-improvement." There's no "ten easy steps" or even a seven-minute TV talk interview. Rather it is a patient unfolding of his personal journey over about five years. He offers himself for your healing, both spiritual and emotional. There is no instant "fix" or cure for the turmoil, sleepless nights, tension when going through the process of divorce. Be patient, read, embrace the nuggets, the insight, and perhaps your move forward may be less painful and more hopeful than Mr. Clark's. God bless.

R. T. Stoddard, Ph.D.

Part One

You're Divorce, the Hurt and Heartache

Done

Being done with a task brings a great feeling of accomplishment, as all your efforts come to a close. Whether it's the yard work on a Saturday, or taking the last test of your college career, it's just a great feeling when you're done. What's not so great is when someone you've been in a relationship with is done with you. You have invested tons of time and resources into making a go of it, only to hear the other party say that they have had enough. That person may come right out and tell you, or maybe they just start shutting down or stop communicating with you altogether. These kinds of circumstances can start you down the path of divorce; the love and communication dries up and one person or both decide that it isn't worth fixing. Then comes the day when your divorce is signed off by the judge and you and your wife are done. It's over, you are married no more, the years of marriage come to a halt, and you pick up the pieces, assess your status and try to move on with your life.

Being done with a marriage comes with its numbing effects; the most pain-inflicting one is the broken heart of rejection. Now

I don't know the reason for your divorce, but you had a hand in it. Doesn't matter what the circumstances were, you still feel the sting of your isolation.

According to John's gospel, chapter 19 verse 30, the last words Jesus uttered as He hung on the cross were, "It is finished!" In other words, Jesus was saying it was done; the Son of God had died for the sins of the world. Now for Jesus, it was His life that came to an end; for you, it was just your marriage. That should give you some perspective; your marriage just ended, not your life.

Now you may not feel like living at the moment. I know that numbing feeling of divorce. I remember the day my ex-wife took the children to the mall so I could gather my things from the house and move out. Being alone in that quiet house, packing my clothes and the things we had agreed that I could take, was a very empty feeling. And then walking out that door for the final time, never to return.… It all still haunts me to this day. What I had to figure out then, and what you have to figure out now, is how to move on from being done. Well, the best thing is to drop the last two letters from "done" and just "do." Whatever the reason for your divorce, whatever caused it, you need to retool yourself and fix some things. Counseling, reading…whatever it takes to move you from being done to being ready to reclaim your life.

If you have children, recognize that you're not totally done when your marriage ends. You may be done being married but you're not done being a dad. That responsibility saved me as my children need me to be there for them; they need me to continue to parent them, even from across town. No matter what it takes, remember you are not done as a parent. Be there for your children.

There may come a point when want to date again. The possibility of rejection will be present in those relationships as well. You will again face the possibility of things not working out no matter how hard you have tried to make it work. My point is that life is a series of ups and downs that call for you to keep looking for direction from the One who suffered and paid the ultimate price for those who rejected Him. Just as Jesus later rose from the dead, so will you as you tie each experience to God's ultimate plan for your life. He does have a plan for your life, and you have to live this life to the end to know it. You can't quit until you're done.

Don't

We are all reminded every day about what we don't do or what we shouldn't do. When we don't do something that is expected, we are letting someone down. When we do something we shouldn't, when we ignore the warning "Don't...," we are breaking a boundary to do something that is forbidden or bad for us. For example, we've all been told, "Don't eat too many greasy foods," because eating a steady diet of these foods is not good for us, not to mention all those calories, so hopefully you have some boundaries in your diet.

Let's talk about expectations that we are failing to meet. As I type this I am listening to one of my favorite love songs. It's a duet by Barbra Streisand and Neil Diamond called "You Don't Bring Me Flowers." Both lovers in this song are singing a list of expectations that the other person is not meeting at this moment in their relationship. It's three minutes of what used to be, both parties realizing some things have changed and they are struggling to hold on to what was once such a good thing. They truly love each other and are remembering all the things they used to do for each other and all the great things they have taught each other.

Barbra begins by singing, "You don't bring me flowers..." Neil replies, "You hardly talk to me anymore..." He doesn't sing her love songs like he used to, and she no longer tells him how much she needs him. If you are a fan of either artist, you can finish the song, but just in case you've forgotten the lyrics, your homework assignment is to go listen to the song and pay attention to the words.

The sadness that reeks from this song is heartbreaking. Look, this song can make your stomach churn because it's a mirror of what may have happened to you and your wife. Your life together started out great, and then the stuff of life crowded out the little things that you used to do for each other. You did a lot of little things to attract her in the first place, and then once she said yes, you quit doing them. Learn anything about that now? Whether it's with your kids or with a new woman you are thinking about dating, you must remember this song and its principles. You have to keep up the practice of doing the little things that communicate your love and concern. Remember, used-to-be's don't count anymore, you have to every day say and do the things that let those around you know that you love and care for them. Say it and do it and you won't have to learn to say the word good-bye ever again.

If God has gifted you with people in your life who are special, then treat them as such. It takes work to continually manage the love that they feel from you; you can't afford weekend breaks in your love for them. John 10 talks about how God has given you this life and asks you to live it abundantly, use His gift, and show others that love. This song can have a different ending, and that ending is up to you. If you don't and never did, then start; if you used to but don't anymore, then start again. It's not that hard to resume doing all the little things that win people's hearts.

Demean

As you move through your divorce, you will have to deal with accusations and half-truths others will tell of what did or didn't happen between you and your ex. Only you and your ex know what really happened, but the rest of the community will be happy to pitch in and fill in the gaps in their story of your life. You may try hard to not talk about it, but trust me; the rest of the town is taking care of that for you.

This part of divorce is the ugly stuff, where everyone gets involved and you are tried in the court of public opinion for your part in the divorce. People talk about you, judge you, accuse you of things that are very far removed from what really happened and who you are. Sure, you would agree that your divorce has your mistakes written all over it, and you know that you own your part in the permanent separation. But the public part of the breaking news has its effect on you, no denying that.

Reminds me of the story found in John 8 of the woman caught in adultery. The Pharisees brought out this woman who was caught in the very act of adultery. They made her stand before Jesus and the crowd that had gathered. They said to Jesus, "Moses commanded us to stone such a woman, now what do you say?" Jesus bent down and wrote in the sand, as they continued to press Him for His answer. As He stood He spoke, "Okay, let anyone of you who is without sin be the first one to cast a stone at her." The scripture says that one by one they dropped their stones and walked away. Jesus asked the woman, "Where are your accusers?" She replied, "Lord, I have no accusers." Jesus then said to her, "Then neither do I accuse you, go and sin no more."

This is a beautiful story of forgiveness and how we should treat one another. Often divorced people are demeaned by others around them. People are so quick to pick up stones and start hurling them your way, when in fact their life is not as squeaky clean as they portray. I know that I didn't feel like defending myself against every accusation or demeaning statement that came my way, so I just learned to turn a deaf ear to it. That was hard to do, but it was necessary to let the truth play out and just trust that everything would eventually come to light, both the good and the bad.

You have got to do the same. You can spend all of your time defending yourself against every little bit of news that has you in it. You have to learn to let it go and trust the Lord that He will defend you from the judgers and accusers who love a juicy story. Own your part of your divorce and when others demean you, just let those rumors and half truths run off your back. I would encourage you to learn that God Himself is the only judge that you need to be concerned about. Jesus asked the woman to go and sin no more, and He did that without jamming her about the very act that she was caught in. So the lesson here is that you may have been guilty in the past, just know that now you are free to go and sin no more. Every day is a chance to do better and conduct yourself in a respectable manner and not get caught up in pleasing everyone around you. God will take care of your accusers. Let Him do that. Meanwhile, you move on and show to others the grace and forgiveness that He has shown you.

Dump

It's usually easy to spot the dump in any city in America: just look for the gulls and crows and follow your nose. It's not a pretty sight as all the stuff that you consider trash gets hauled out of your house to the garbage bin. Then once a week you take the bin to the curb (if you don't forget) and all your trash gets hauled away to the dump. The trash you dump in the bin is stuff that isn't useful to you anymore. You drink the final bit of milk from the plastic container and then throw the container away because it's now useless; the milk is gone and the container has served its purpose. You grow weary or grow out of your clothes or shoes, so you gather them and take them to Goodwill because you are done with them; they don't fit anymore or don't suit you anymore. My point is that we are quick to throw trash away or give away an article of clothing but we cling to thoughts and beliefs and habits that we should have dumped months or years ago.

In Philippians 3:13, Paul says, "But I focus on this one thing, forgetting the past and looking forward to what lies ahead." One thing that will delay your recovery from your divorce will be your inability to forget some things and move on. The stress and drama that comes with a divorce, not to mention the life-changing decisions that now shape your new life, is maddening. The amount of anger and resentment is enough to choke a horse, and if you are not careful you will carry that with you far too long. It's normal to feel those emotions and others when you're in the trenches of divorce, but you don't want to stay there. The sleepless nights, all the "what if" scenarios you continue to play through in your head… they will make you crazy if you don't get a handle on them.

Divorces tend to drive your friends and those you used to run with away from you. That's what makes it so tough to deal with all these thoughts; without the perspective of another person, it's too easy to just let it all play through your mind, all the time. It is so important that you find a trusted pastor or counselor you can develop a relationship with so you can begin to sort through these thoughts. Some thoughts and feelings will provide a foundation on which you can now start to build your new life. You will be able to recognize your past mistakes and your weaknesses so you can work on them as you recover. Also recognize that there are some feelings and beliefs you need to dump. If God forgives you, then you need to forgive yourself. God also says that after He forgives, He forgets. You need to do likewise, and start to forget some of what has happened to you. You will have enough of this experience that will want to follow you the rest of your life, but I believe that you can start now to practice forgetfulness.

The above-referenced scripture says that Paul put his past behind him and was now pressing on toward his future. You need to do the same and start dumping the garbage from your mind and memory. If it's old and useless and doesn't suit you anymore, it's got to go—you need to hit the delete button and dump this harmful memory. No one I know hangs around the dump, and neither should you. Back up, dump it and drive off.

Duel

Being a fan of Wild West movies, I have seen my share of Main Street duels. Usually it's the good guy and the bad guy at opposite ends of the street in a feud-ending showdown. Some problem has escalated beyond repair and the only way to settle it is to shoot it out. Depending on the ending there is usually one survivor, and the other body is dragged off to be buried.

Webster calls a duel "a prearranged fight," and in most divorces that is exactly what it is. Unresolved problems continue to boil with no resolution and the two parties resort to name calling instead of working it out. Lines are drawn and then someone says that they are done; usually that person is the first to lawyer up. We now have a once happily married couple acting like they are mortal enemies, and with friends choosing sides, blood starts to boil.

It's amazing. The two who couldn't stop talking while they were dating now don't talk. Back then they could not wait to be married so they could live together, and now they can't stand to be in the same room. It's like a duel: They start to march toward opposite ends of the spectrum and the tension builds till the shooting starts. The street has cleared of bystanders, yet everyone attached to the couple watches from safe places. When the two stop walking apart and turn to face each other, it's time to see who will shoot first. This part can seem to take forever or it can happen in a heartbeat—it really depends on the emotion or drama related to the causes.

The stark contrast between a duel and a divorce is that in a duel, someone usually gets shot and dies, while in a divorce both parties lose without a shot being fired. A divorce hearing can be the most mean-spirited, vengeful event in a courtroom. The hurtful accusations and intentional pain the once loving couple inflict on each other are almost unimaginable. Leveraging children, money and possessions to punish the other is all justified in minds that at one time said "until death do us part." In this battle the parties don't attract anymore; they are like magnets, where the like poles fight each other and refuse attraction.

My counsel to you men who are standing at the end of your Main Street facing your ex is to drop your pistol and start walking toward your issues. If you and your ex draw down on each other you can assure yourself of being in the bull's-eye of her and her attorney. Your ability to make things as peaceful as possible will serve you in the long run. Every situation is different and you need to seek peace at every point possible. Honor God with your reasoning and decision making, trusting Him to create a best possible outcome for you. This isn't fun, but it's now part of your life and you need to treat it as you would any big decision. Fact finding and letting go of any anger or emotion will cause you to be less hasty and more practical in this very intense time.

This isn't the Wild West, and you can't walk out of this movie just because you don't like the storyline. The only way to survive this duel is to trust God with it and with you. Proverbs 15:1: "A gentle answer turns away wrath, but a harsh word stirs up anger."

DRIFT

IF YOU'RE IN A POOL on your favorite floating device sipping the cold beverage of your choice, the word *drift* has a pleasant meaning for you as you relax and float without a care. To others the word *drift* is a scary term as it means that you are not on course, you have strayed and are no longer headed toward where you intended to land or finish. Things can drift as wind, ocean currents, or storms all play with their course and send them away from their intended destination. Think of a man in a rowboat who loses his oars and gets caught in a current, drifting far out to sea instead of heading back toward shore. Different circumstances or events can cause us to drift: a poor relationship, a child who is not on track, a pressure-packed job or the loss of that job. The death of a close friend or family member can also cause us to drift.

A divorce can cause us to drift off the course that we were on for sure. Years ago, if you had told me that I would be divorced after eighteen years of marriage, I would have laughed at you. My then-spouse and I had struggles just like every other marriage, but I never saw the divorce coming. We think that we have it all figured out, that things are going to turn out just like we've planned: the kids will grow up and leave home, and you and your wife will grow old together. My story will now have a different ending than the one that I had planned out for myself, and the same may be true for you as well. Funny how life takes its twists and turns, and if we are not careful these unplanned events can really mess us up.

Just as the influence of alcohol can at times cause a drunk driver to drift into oncoming traffic, the influence of your divorce can cause you to drift as well. When I talk about you drifting, I am speaking to you leaving the core beliefs and character that you once embraced. The drifting can start well before the divorce as you try to keep the peace in a family that is full of turmoil. You may be the very cause of that turmoil, and not your ex-wife; I am not here to decide that. But someone is drifting or has drifted from what they promised on your wedding day.

Take this time of being single to chart out a new course for yourself. It may be that you need to check and challenge the core beliefs that you had and now have, if you find they are not working or producing the results that you want. If so, I would ask you to do some soul searching and come up with a game plan for change. Seven years after my divorce, I still see my counselor once a month. Our conversations have changed over the years, but his wisdom and insight are invaluable to me as I am continuing to change for the better. I have had to confess some wrong thinking and shed some ways of behaving, and now I am seeing the positive changes in the things I am investing my time in.

What you need to stop the drifting is a rudder to give your life direction. Humbling yourself to God is the rudder you need. 1 Peter, chapter 5 verse 10 says, "After you have suffered for a little while, the God of all grace, who called you to His eternal glory in Christ, will Himself perfect, confirm, strengthen and establish you." Now your part in that verse is to submit yourself to the will of God and get out of the way. Stop the drifting and align yourself under the will of God for your life. Find a trusted friend to keep you accountable with your changes and regularly plot your results against your newly chosen course. If you find that you're drifting, correct it this time; have the courage to do what is necessary to achieve your goals. My favorite quote says that if you don't know where you're going, any road will take you there. Be determined to say no to things that would cause you to drift; stay on target and on time with the new course you have or will choose. Get my drift?

Drag

This word gives you the mental picture of taking something or someone to someplace against their will. The idea of someone dragging you to court, for example, or maybe the thought of going to court can be a drag. If someone does not like technology, often we say that we are going to drag them into the twenty-first century. We often have to drag things mentally as well as physically to get them where we want them. That's one sense of the word *drag*, but the use of this word that I want to discuss with you is "dragging things out," as in when we avoid issues in our lives and let them become big things—things that become a drag on us and our families. Our refusal to deal with things allows them to linger in our hearts and minds, dragging us down. Instead of facing our problems or issues head-on, we just hope that they will go away all by themselves. That almost never happens!

Addictions play a role in some marriages that end in divorce. We have seen gambling force families apart, along with the easy access to alcohol and drugs. These actions start out in secret until the warning signs of the addiction spill over into erratic public behavior. Porn is a silent killer of marriages as the addicted one can't get enough of the visual stimulation and often escalates to prostitution. A side effect of all of these addictions is physical and mental abuse of a marriage partner, when the behavior becomes uncontrollable and the addict doesn't want to be told that they have a problem.

I don't know if I have just touched on a land mine as far as you're concerned, but if you are under the influence of one of these demons, don't wait to be dragged in for treatment. You have already seen this destroy your marriage, and next in line for demolition will be you if you don't get some help. You first have to recognize that you are having a hard time with this addiction and that you can't kick it by yourself. Stop lying to yourself, telling yourself it's not that bad, when everyone around you is screaming at you to get help. If you let this drag on and on, you will see your finances start to erode as you have to foot the bill for the ever-increasing habit that will eventually break you and take every dime you have. Not to mention the danger you put yourself in daily, and if you are using, the danger you put your children in at your home or when you are driving them in your car. You never think it's as bad as it really is until something happens and suddenly your circumstances catch up with your actions. Next thing you know you lose your driver's license and spend some time in jail for a DUI, and now you can't get to work or go get your kids when it's your weekend.

If you are reading this page and dealing with an addiction, I beg you to go get some professional help. Most employers have insurance plans that will allow you to submit yourself to treatment on a voluntary basis with no penalty to you, because you initiated the treatment. It's a totally different story if you are caught in a random drug screen by your company and you test positive. Before you drag your existing children and family into your cycle of abuse, just know that God wants to deliver you from your demons. Call on His name today and ask Him in prayer to rescue you from yourself and lead you to a full recovery and healthy lifestyle.

Down

I know that there are times in this divorce process when you get knocked down. Just when you thought that it couldn't get any worse…it gets worse. I can think back on many sleepless nights away from my children when I didn't think I could go on another day. Just the thought of my children living in another man's house was unbearable. After all, they were my children, not his, but I was powerless to do anything about it. I still had my weekend visits, but having just two days out of seven begins to take its toll on your brain and heart after a few short months. So I know how it feels to be down and maybe close to being out as well.

In Psalm 55 verse 22, God tells us to cast our burdens upon Him, "and He will sustain you." You might say God is asking you to lay your burdens down, if you will. Give them to Him; let Him fight your battles for you. That might come as a strange thought to you as you read this, because you may have never let anyone fight for you your whole life long. There are some battles that just belong with the Lord and not with you. Once your divorce is final, there is little you can do to change the agreement you just signed your name to. No matter how fair or unfair you view your circumstances, God can see the whole picture better than you ever will. The scripture in Genesis says that He spoke the stars into existence and was involved in the creation of the world as we know it; surely He is powerful enough to help you in your time of need.

Your need may be in the realm of children, finances, or just your state of mind. I would encourage you to unsaddle yourself from all of your worries and give them to God. For me the need was in my heart; it just hurt all the time and I could not get over the magnitude of my loss. Not living with my children was the most devastating thing that anyone can go through. It wasn't what I wanted, but I could not stop the domino effect of the actions of my ex-spouse. It finally came down to me just crying out to the Lord and asking Him to help me deal with all of my hurt. I can't tell you that I immediately felt better, but I did slowly become aware that I had to turn my hurt into a positive action and make the best of my plight. I began to really focus on my communication with my children, on the phone, texting them and when I had them with me. I began to see that I was getting to know my children at an accelerated pace that might never have happened had we all still lived together as a family.

Your heart may still be hurting and your tears may still be running down your face, but let me tell you that it does get better. It gets better when you decide to deal with what you have been dealt or agreed to and start finding ways to improve yourself and your circumstances. God stands ready to take your burdens from you and free you up to trust Him to fight your battles for you. You do all you can do and let Him do the supernatural, and then watch your hurt start to manifest into something positive that you can get excited about. Be determined to survive this and to come out of it blessed beyond your wildest imagination. You may be down, but it's not over until God says it's over. I can tell you from personal experience that God will come to your rescue if you will let go of all the anger and bitterness and hurt that may still linger in your heart. Once you rid yourself of those destructive emotions, God can fill you with positive energy and thought to start your comeback. Being down is just a state of mind. It's time to pick yourself up and let God fight your battles and carry your burdens.

Here is a blank page for you to capture those life changing thoughts from the pages you have just read...

Dodge

At first this word may trigger thoughts of grade school dodge ball, or maybe a make of car or truck in your or your neighbor's driveway. Webster uses a phrase that really sums up the meaning I became most familiar with after my divorce: "Avoid by so moving." I know that after I became divorced I avoided people; I learned how to dodge anyone and everyone I thought I would run into in public places.

Now that may not sound like you, but for me I would go to great lengths to not be seen by my friends or the acquaintances of my ex-wife. I was hurting from the trauma of the whole experience of having my family torn apart, I was missing my children and my living situation was now different. Everything was different. My ex-wife and I had been to all the places where we had done business together as a couple and notified them of our divorce; everything was now separated and we told the story over and over to the bank, doctors' offices, insurance…you get the picture.

In my situation I had to go live in a spare bedroom in my widowed mother's home. I left my former life with just my car and my clothes and took residence up with my mom. That event was devastating! It was at that point that I began to just hide from everyone. I would go to the grocery store at 10 p.m. so I would not be seen by anyone. I never stopped going to church, but for sure I was on the back row, in late and the first to leave. I didn't want to be seen by anyone, and if I was ever cornered by a friend I felt so uneasy and small. They would always ask, "How are you doing?" But I had nothing positive to say and usually gave a less than enthusiastic response. I just had a hard time getting over the fact that my marriage was over and I was by myself. Your mind and circumstances have a way of forcing you out of your most positive thoughts. I also remember the hollowest feeling in the pit of my stomach, a pain that just would not go away. After eighteen years of a marriage that had both good and bad times, I would at that moment have traded anything just to belong to my family again, but that was a long-gone possibility.

I don't know how you handled the first few days and weeks of your divorce, but I can sure sympathize with those of you who dodged everyone, not wanting to be seen in public. It's hard to deal with the pain and you just don't feel like talking about it. So you pull away from everyone, even your best friends; you just want your kids on their visits and a place to hide. If you are facing that battle right now, I trust that you will listen to me for a few sentences. The pain is real but it does get better; you will one day venture out and see that you can exist in public again and grow into your new life. Divorce happens too much these days, and you are neither the first nor the last to have these feelings. Let God remind you that He has you in the palm of His hand and if you will let Him, He will restore you and set your feet on solid ground again. It's this solid ground that will allow you to stop dodging and start living again.

DNA

ARE YOU HOOKED ON ONE of the many *CSI* shows that are now on television? Take your pick: there's one set in Miami and Vegas and now even New York. The criminal justice field has been turned upside down by the advances in DNA research and technology. Criminal cases that had gone cold years ago are now opened again with DNA testing that can put the guilty behind bars. Inmates who had been on death row have walked free from prison after new scientific tests concluded that they didn't do the crime.

Going through my divorce really rocked me. I had invested eighteen years in a marriage and it was undone with three signatures. My identity was all wrapped up in who I was as a dad and a husband and a sales manager. All three parts of my identity were shaken to the core with the news that my spouse and I were no longer going to be married.

Do you feel that way? The key for you to understand as you go through this process is that you are you. You are part of many things in your life, and we attach ourselves to many relationships and duties, but over time we forget who we are. We get so used to caring for everyone else and giving ourselves to lots of causes that the person in the mirror becomes virtually invisible and unrecognizable. That is why I was so mangled after my divorce: I was separated from so many things I had become attached to that, now alone, I didn't recognize myself without all the stuff that had been in my life.

My appeal to you is to start the practice of caring for yourself; take steps to make sure that you are cared for, even if you are the only one doing it. Now that you're on your own for this period of time, use this space to reach deep inside and get to know the person that God made you to be. I found that I really love photography, and now my house is full of pictures that I have taken and framed. I also found out that I like to write, where before I never, ever, thought that I had the patience to pound out my thoughts on a keyboard. These newfound discoveries about myself didn't spill out in the first weeks after my divorce, but as time passed and I searched for peace and happiness, I found myself doing and being what I wanted to do and be. This really brought a new sense of freedom to now explore even further into my innermost thoughts and desires. As I write this page, almost seven years post-divorce, I am still discovering things about myself that cause me both pain and pleasure. I am a work in progress, and the scripture that comes to mind is Philippians 1 verse 6. It states that, "He who began a good work in you will perfect it until the day of Christ Jesus."

If you have Jesus in your life, and are yielding to Him, there is a process through which you can allow Him to help you with this transformation. He is not going to bully you around and turn you into a hermit; rather He will take who you are and start the perfection process of turning you into the man that God wants and created you to be. Yielding is the key to seeing this transformation and getting a look at the blueprint God had intended for your life. Your DNA is God given; it's who you are and who you were created to be and it's alive in you right now. You're not a crime scene; you are a child of the most high God. Now go discover what makes you so unique.

Division

WEBSTER DEFINES THIS WORD AS "being divided or the process of being divided." The word picture that comes to mind is the dividing of a tiny cell under the microscope. The once singular cell goes through a process and then becomes two cells. Another example of division is when our children graduate from high school and then move away to college or take a job and we move them into their first apartment—that's division. One more example that I would share would be a section of scripture, Acts 15:39, where Paul and Barnabas were deciding whether to take Mark with them as they were thinking about going back to visit some of the places where they had preached the word of God. In verse 39, "There arose such a sharp disagreement that they separated from one another and Barnabas took Mark with him and sailed away."

In your divorce you have experienced division from your former spouse, and you may be saddened by that, or you may be relieved, whatever the case may have been. But the one piece of division that may catch you off guard is the division from your ex-spouse's family. In the years that you were married you may have built some very strong relationships with your ex's parents or siblings. Those relationships may now have begun to fade away due to some changed circumstances, but the largest change is that you are no longer part of their family. It gets even more complicated if you have children who are still tied to that family as grandchildren and nephews and nieces. They get to go over for special occasions and holidays but you don't; you get to drop them off and then go pick them up. You used to go up to the front door and walk in and be welcomed with hugs and kisses, now you wave from your car from the driveway. Then you return home to a very quiet house and become consumed by the thought of all the loss you continue to experience.

The only comfort I can give you here is to understand that this kind of division just happens. I personally did and still do love my in-laws very much, but now that I am divorced from their daughter we have moved apart. I still see them at ball games and public events and we exchange pleasantries, but that is about it. Remember that blood is thicker than water, meaning that they will always choose their daughter over you, regardless of what happened.

Don't waste your energy stewing about issues that you can't change and that don't matter now. Start accepting the fact that you are not a part of that family anymore and move on. Start caring less and less about all that you used to know about that family and use that energy to focus on you. You are now on a different path, one that will day by day take you further and further away from what used to be. You can still say hello and be nice when you see your former in-laws, but don't get sucked back into their life. You have enough problems of your own that need your attention. You may choose not to sit on the same set of bleachers with them at your child's ball game, and that is okay. It still may hurt a little, but remember the reality of the situation. You are not a part of their family anymore.

DIVIDE

I CAN REMEMBER PLAYING MARBLES ON the dirt surface in the back alley of my neighborhood until it was so dark we had to quit. One day my friend was so upset at losing that he gathered up all of his marbles and left us, stomping off headed back to his house. That is a pretty good word picture of what happens in a divorce.

After a marriage of a few years or a few decades you now have the daunting task of dividing up all of your assets. You now go from having joint checking and savings accounts to each of you having your own separate accounts. Furniture, toys, investments… you both take turns trading lists of what you want and what you need. The worst for me was the pictures of our family and the children. I left without them and was only allowed to get copies under supervision of the attorney's office. I had to tell the lady which pictures I wanted and then had to pay to have copies made of the ones I picked out. That was really hard for me as I sat there going through our family memories, picture by picture, and then to be supervised just to look at pictures of my own kids…I guess they thought I might steal a picture or something. I am sure that you have your own painful memory of dividing your stuff and it's not something you ever want relive or do again.

I don't know what's harder, parting company or parting with some of your belongings. Some divorces are civil and the decisions on who gets what are made without much disagreement. But some divorces are knock-down drag-outs that involve accountants and attorneys and may go on for months. As you read this work I am not sure what you have just been through or are going through, but I can know with some certainty that it was painful to divide the family's assets. Others who have not gone through a divorce may claim that it's just stuff and ask what the big deal is anyway. Well, the big deal is that all that stuff was bought in a family setting; it all carries memories and documents time in your marriage.

The other aspect of dividing the assets is that you both have to go on now, in separate directions. Things like cash, retirement, pension plans, and 401k accounts all come into play, so I hope you had a good attorney and came away in good shape. I have known men and women who were so distraught about the divorce or that the other side made it so difficult, they just walked away because they wouldn't or couldn't go through the trauma and the fighting anymore.

The opposite of divide is to multiply. Now comes the exciting part of your recovery, and I believe that it comes in many different areas. Ephesians 3 verse 20 says, "Now to Him who is able to do exceeding abundantly beyond all that we ask or think, according to the power that works within us." God has the power to restore you in all areas of your life, including emotional, intellectual and monetary. I know that some of you are still hurting from your divorce, but just know that you can rebuild your life and wealth in the days ahead. Take care of yourself, your children, and do the right things always as you step into your new life's direction. Trust God, let Him work on you and satisfy your needs and He will span the great divide.

DISTANCE

THERE IS NOTHING LIKE A divorce to give you the feeling of distance. Distance from your ex-spouse, distance from his/her family, and distance from the life you once knew. The feeling of being detached and now floating away from a life that you thought would only end at the death of you or your spouse. But what died was not your spouse, it was your marriage, and that is a death that just won't let go. Every day you are reminded of what used to be and what could have been, and you are faced with "What now?"

Well, where will you go? What will you do? If there are children, you may be haunted by thoughts of how they are going to process their parents' split. All these thoughts have you asking questions that will be answered by time. With the passing of time comes the reality that with each day you create distance from what was your family and marriage and now starts the pilgrimage to what will be. The question of distance can't be answered until you ask yourself, "Where do I want to go?"

Is a move in your plans? Or will you need to go back to college to finish that degree because the burden of being the breadwinner now falls squarely upon your shoulders? So two thoughts now converge on the blank piece of paper: where do you want to start and how long will it take you to get there? You can have many destinations as you navigate the distance to your goal, but remember that life needs to be lived every day in between. It's easy to get excited about your newly found freedom and set lofty, noble goals, but those goals may take many months and maybe years to accomplish. Also, some goals really have no clear answer of how they're going to come about. You may want to one day get married again, but at the moment you have no one in mind. Others may be easier to define, like enrolling with a counselor to help you recover from the trauma of your divorce. You'll need both short-term and long-terms goals; the short-term ones are there to give you a sense of accomplishment, and the long-term ones will give you purpose. Be sure as you write your goals to do so with a pencil, as they will most likely change many times as you re-create yourself and your life.

Let's finish with the thought of putting Humpty Dumpty back together again. This divorce, no matter how civil or how devastating, has left hurts and scars. With some professional help, you need to get in touch with the new you that will emerge. You will not be the same person going forward; you will change and go through many new things in the coming months and years. Along the way you will discover passions and desires and also areas of pain you never knew you had. Please, no passing on the pain; deal with it, and understand yourself and process it. You need to walk that path and get the attention and care that will be the foundation for your new life. Time and distance and hard work will produce a changed life. No shortcuts or detours, please. Walk the path.

Disappear

When you say this word audibly, you get the flashbacks of watching your favorite magician on television making people or things disappear. David Copperfield and others make their living by creating illusions that would have you think that folks have disappeared from covered boxes the magician has spun around a few times. A little hocus-pocus and remove the drape from the once spinning box and we expel our breath wondering, "Just how did he do that?"

In a divorce, there are a few things that we would love to shove in a spinning box and make disappear—can I get a witness on that! All the big and small things start to get divided, and questions start being asked about your most private affairs. Your personal life and assets are all out in the open for others, not you, to decide who gets what. Depending on the length of your marriage, you might see lots of your things disappear as they get slid over into your ex-spouse's column. Its one thing to have your money disappear, but quite another to have your privacy disappear. All of your financial records, tax returns, retirement and your 401k are now in the hands of those who get paid to divide everything you have worked for. Every bit of personal information that might be of interest is now requested and examined.

While your assets are important and precious to you, I want to talk about something else that is more valuable than the abovementioned stuff. The reason I used the word "stuff" is that most if not all of it can be replaced. You can make more money, you can start another investment account—all that stuff might disappear for a while, but it can be acquired again. But there are a few things that are a little harder to make disappear. Those would be the haunting things that we have all done that we wish we could have back. Perhaps one of those things was the final straw that brought on the divorce. A pattern of destructive behavior that you just have a hard time shaking may be on your list of things that you need to disappear. Whatever sin it is that just hounds you as you try to put this divorce behind you, God can make it disappear. How, you ask?

Psalm 103 verse 12 says, "As far as the east is from the west, so far has he removed our transgressions/sins from us." Imagine a globe for a moment. If you start from your hometown and head north, you will cross the top of the globe and begin to head south—follow me? Now if you head east from your hometown, you just continue to head east; east never becomes west. The distance between the east and west is infinite. So when God removes your sins from you as far as the east is from the west, He separates your sins from you as far as infinite is from infinite—how wonderful is that? Now add one more verse to this, I John 1:9, which says, "If we confess our sins, He is faithful and righteous to forgive us our sins and to cleanse us from all unrighteousness." Now it's up to you to ask God to forgive you and experience this total forgiveness. With this forgiveness comes a change in behavior. Forgiveness is not a revolving door where you ask for forgiveness and then keep right on sinning. God's ability to forgive is no magic act; He really can make your sin disappear!

Displaced

In a natural disaster many homes are destroyed. Floods, tornados and hurricanes leave thousands homeless each year. Years after Hurricane Katrina, we still had Louisiana families living in other states or in government housing. Over the past several years our economy has displaced singles and families alike, with jobs disappearing due to the uncertainty we face in the marketplace.

You might say the greatest storm that you have faced to date was your divorce. I can remember my own displacement: One day I am living in a 4,000-square-foot house with a pool and a basketball court, and the next day I am walking out the door with just my clothes and some personal belongings. I went from my home to the spare bedroom in my mother's house across town. That first night alone was the most haunting experience of my life; I was not with my children, not in my home and not in my bed. I was displaced. I remember trying to go to the post office to secure a box, and I could not get one because I didn't have a physical address to reference. At forty-seven years of age, I had to have my mother sign for me to be able to get a post office box. That was one of the lowest points in my post-divorce life. I was so displaced and broken, everything I had was stripped away and I was really struggling.

That existence lasted for twenty-two months. After a job change I was able to afford a three-bedroom unfurnished apartment. I remember buying a sleeping bag so I could spend the first night in my new apartment. I had nothing: no dishes, bed, towels…nothing. Slowly I began to furnish my apartment with secondhand pieces of furniture and a card table that doubled as a work desk and a meal table when my children came over to visit. Finally I had a home where I could be with my children alone. It took me almost two years to have that, and boy did it feel good. I spent one year in that apartment and then bought the home that I am in today.

I don't know your story of displacement or if you had to leave your home or not, but you don't have to be homeless to be displaced. The mental displacement can be a real killer, as you may feel as I did, that all those years of marriage have been flushed down the toilet. Your routine has stopped, your family is across town—now what? What do you do with yourself? You're all alone and in your mind and heart it gets real quiet. All the chatter of children and the rush at mealtime is gone; you are not a part of bath time and chasing children into bed anymore at the house you once lived in. I truly missed all of that, and you can never replace it with anything.

I can assure you that God sees everything and knows what you're going through. Psalm 138 verse 8 says, "The Lord will accomplish what concerns me; Thy loving-kindness, O Lord, is everlasting." Deal with your displacement by spending every moment you can with your children, and when you are alone, keep busy with productive things that will serve you well as you rebuild your life. Yes, I know there will be hard days and nights of loneliness and despair. I would have handy the phone numbers of trusted friends who can help pick you up as you deal with your loss and displacement.

As time passed for me, life became more manageable and I was able to replace most of the things that I was displaced from. The things that can never be taken from you are your dignity and hope. Hold strong and maintain a healthy lifestyle and positive mental attitude. You can't spend a lot of time wondering what happened. A friend of mine once said, "Don't put a question mark where God has put a period." The meaning here is that, for some reason, God has allowed this divorce to happen. He is in control, so start moving forward, trusting Him to show you His best, and know that your divorce is not the end of you, it's just what happened to you.

Disorder

Leading up to and through your divorce, there is lots of disorder. A lifetime of organization and planning with your former spouse has now begun to unravel. You find yourself paying an attorney to untangle your once happy marriage. And the longer the marriage the harder it is to sort through the accumulated assets and property that now have to be divided up between the two of you.

The disorder can continue in your head and in your body as well. In your head the once daily routine is now splintered with newfound responsibilities that you may in the past have allowed your spouse to handle. Now that you're living apart, your sense of purpose may have hit the skids, and you find yourself battling depression or very high anxiety. These mental companions are enough to cause you to think that you're losing your mind. That is why many times in this book I have encouraged you to get professional counseling to help guide you through the mental minefield that divorce can cause. No matter how strong you think you are, I can tell you with absolute confidence that your mental recovery will be slowed and compromised if you try to do it all alone.

Your body can become affected by the sudden or prolonged disorder of your mind; it may show up in weight gain or weight loss. Maybe you stop eating or you can't control your appetite as you try to use food to fill your lack of comfort. You also stop going out and exercising. All you want to do is rehash everything that has happened to you and rationalize the predicament you find yourself in. You hide from the public and do your grocery shopping at 10 p.m. and your wardrobe may only consist of things that have elastic in the waistline. You may also have let your personal hygiene drop a notch as you convince yourself that nobody wants you now. I have mentioned some extremes here, but you get the picture of how your life of disorder can produce some unwanted and previously unseen pictures of you.

The best response to disorder is to deal with it and turn the tables on this feeling of confusion. With your counselor you can now plot a way through the new life you have been handed. You can take the muddled mess and start to assemble the pieces. Start with forgiving whoever you need to forgive and removing all the hurt that will not let you move on. This baggage has prolonged more divorce recoveries than I care to mention. Forgive and forget and let's move on in a direction of positive thoughts and results. You can't change what happened in the past, but you can certainly have a say about your remaining days on planet earth. You may still have unanswered questions about the past, and truthfully you may never get your questions answered this side of heaven. But tomorrow is begging to be lived. You need to reverse course and change the disorder into order. Take control of what you can control and leave the rest to God as He is in charge of the supernatural. You can do it, so get started and let's get going in an orderly fashion.

Disgust

Have you ever been disgusted? Webster calls disgust "a sickening dislike," and you can probably recall things or situations that have disgusted you. Your stomach begins to turn and you feel your skin crawl as you don't want to watch anymore or you feel the need to leave the room. In fact you now know and can make a list of things that disgust you. Disgust may have changed what kind of situations you allow yourself to be put in or be a part of.

Do you know that God gets disgusted? In Proverbs 6 verses 16-19 the writer lists seven things that the Lord hates, or seven things that disgust Him: haughty eyes, lying, killing, a heart that devises wicked plans, feet that run toward evil, false witness and someone that spreads gossip.

This page is not put here to beat you up but rather to give you a place to start as you recover from your divorce. I have no doubt that you have been through the mill with stuff and people and attorneys, but now we need to take a mop and clean out the room where all of this took place. From this mess you are going to keep very little. Most of your thoughts and who you were in your marriage will need an overhaul. So let's back up the dumpster and start pitching out what we don't need and things that disgust us. To do that efficiently you will need a professional counselor to help you sort through the remains of who you were as a married person. Now that you have the time and desire to bounce back, start to rebuild yourself into whom God created you to be.

I will now come back to the things that disgust God, because as you rebuild yourself you need to do that reconstruction in the word of God. In your divorce, you played a part in the eventual separation of you and your spouse. No one is perfect, but more is better when it comes to the knowledge of what God desires and what disgusts Him. The new you can be so attractive and winsome and that attraction will come from you allowing the love of God to come shining through your new heart. Reading the scripture, attending church, and developing a positive group of friends is a good start. Prayer is where you talk to God and you get to listen Him talk back to you. As you begin this journey of getting to know the heart of God, you will begin to embrace the fruits of the Spirit as they are listed in Galatians 5:22. Love, joy, peace, patience, kindness, goodness and self-control will all infuse themselves into you as you commit yourself to the word of God.

This change won't come overnight and will probably come with a few setbacks, but don't lose heart. You're on the mend, and you need to allow yourself to heal and time to consider who you want to be and square that with who God wants you to be. Funny thing about walking with the Savior, His wants and desires for you will soon become yours as well. It's time to get excited and ready for the ride of your life as you begin to change and embrace a new way of thinking and living. Begin to journal and log your progress toward the new creation that you and your time with the Lord will create. Time to forget the past hurts and embrace your very bright future. One step at a time, one day at a time—that is how you do it.

Here is a blank page for you to capture those life changing thoughts from the pages you have just read...

Dilemma

It's always great to want something new, but after that feeling of wanting comes the choosing. If you were a born shopper, then you're in paradise, but even then depending on the situation you can just become overwhelmed with the choices. What size? What color? If it isn't in stock, should I wait for it or choose something else? These are all decisions that you get to make as you consider your purchase.

What a dilemma: up or down, in or out, come or go—you get the picture. Or how about night or day, summer or winter, spring or fall, early or late, boy or girl, cat or dog—even more to consider. Your life might have been pretty routine up until the divorce proceeding came upon you. Now you are just swamped with decisions. What attorney to choose, what holidays do you want your children, and who gets what. I am telling you that this can just wear you out, because what you choose is what you get to live with for a very long time. What makes it even tougher is that you have to talk with your ex through an attorney, and every conversation costs you money.

Another choice that you get to make is, are you going to date again and consider getting married again at some point in time? Some men just can't wait to get out and replace all this hurt with another relationship. I have known some guys who start dating before the papers have even been signed. I don't want to be the dating police here, but let me throw out some considerations for you to think about. First, if you have children, I would ask you to hold off on dating for a while and pour all of your attention on your children. They don't need another woman to deal with at this point... they need you! They need your strength and security, for you to do your best to let them know that they are going to be all right. Your children are your first priority as you emerge from the divorce; help them adjust by being available to be with them anytime you can.

Second, you have a dilemma to solve: What do you want now? You know what you had in your marriage, but what about now, what do you want? I have stressed that you need to get into some kind of counseling so you can mend internally from your divorce. The reason that that gets to be part of your formula for dating again is because your next mate deserves better, just like you do, right? You will not be very attractive to be around if all you do is talk about your ex and rehash old conflicts that your new date doesn't know or care anything about.

You have to also pray and ask God to direct you in this process. It's tough to date again, at forty or fifty, or whatever age you are; it seems like fun until you're in it. By this time in life we are all entrenched in our behaviors and what you see is what you will get. The dating, the rejection and all that communicating...that is the headwind you must face if you are looking for that one right person. Lots of women want to be taken care of, and then there are those who are convinced that they don't need a man. You have to sift through that list and find the package that has your name on it. The dilemma I hope you will have settled in your mind is that you will take God on this new journey.

Dignity

As you go through your day you are constantly observing folks, making judgments about them or the circumstances they are in. I know that sounds bad, but I don't mean just picking a person apart with your words. The judgments I am talking about come with seeing those around us who need us to step in and help them, those who may be struggling to maintain their dignity in the face of some pretty tough circumstances. Single moms who are running children everywhere and then barely make it to work on time, or perhaps single moms who need assistance just to feed their children. Or a newly divorced man who maybe needs a place to live if he's been forced to relocate from the home he once lived in.

Let me first say to the divorced man who is reading this page, going through a divorce is nothing to hang your head about. I know that your heart may hurt and you now have a whole new set of issues to work through, but you can still have your dignity. No judge or ex-spouse can take that away from you, unless you give it to them. You can still put your shoulders back and make a comeback. I don't know what happened in your marriage that caused you to now be a single man, but whatever it is, it can be forgiven by God and you can recover from it. As a married couple you and your ex had your friends, and those friends may have chosen sides through your divorce, maybe saying or doing things that can sting a little. But I am asking you to set all that aside and let the love of God shine through.

Through this process of healing, God is going to send people to help you in many ways. You need to be okay with that, as God will use others to come to your rescue. If you're too proud to receive their help, you are actually saying no to God and yes to your sinful pride. God will speak to those around you and give them insight into what you need. He has already blessed them with resources to help you. The help may come in the form of money, a place to live, or helping you with your kids while you have to work some overtime. You still can maintain your dignity and receive assistance from others. I know it's going to go against your grain to accept gifts of time or money from others and you may feel like a charity case, but you need to see what is actually happening. God is answering your prayers through others to bless you and them. They get blessed by saying yes to Him as they are prompted to give and actually do so; you get blessed as the gifts match up with the prayers that you have been praying. Again you have to get out of the way when God is working and let Him work through others to help you in your time of need.

The other blessing you can receive is that after you have recovered from your divorce you can now help other men who need assistance after their divorce. Now you know what they are feeling and you can help. You can come alongside them and coach them to keep their heads up and advise them on how to handle the many issues that you know are coming down the pike. Money will be spent and hugs may wear off, but dignity is the trait that can quicken the recovery time of a divorced male. If someone gave your dignity back to you, make sure that you do the same with someone else.

Dice

Just the mention of the word *dice* makes you think of gambling or your favorite board game. The sides are numbered from one to six and just a toss can determine your fate in your favorite game. The trouble with dice is that they're used in games of chance, meaning that the dice determine your outcome and it really has nothing to do with you.

Let's talk about the children of divorce. Your divorce has turned your children's world upside down. If you as a married person didn't come from a divorced family, then you are very much unaware of the situation you have just put your children in. The two people who brought these precious souls into the world now can't stand to be in the same room together. I can remember the cry out of the mouth of one of my children as I asked her if she wanted to go with her mom or stay with me. She said, "Dad, I am tired of choosing between you and Mom!" That hit me like a ton of bricks as I had not realized the pressure that our divorce put on them then, and it even plays out today, seven years later. You may feel relieved at not having your ex-spouse around anymore, but your joy should be tempered as you now see the trick box that you have put your children in. You get your peace, so to speak, but meanwhile your children get stuck in between you and your ex while their feelings and sense of security get shuffled like a deck of cards. You have moved from a marriage/ family relationship to a court-settled contract on how the custody of your children will be carried out. We are not talking about who gets the big-screen TV; rather we are talking about your flesh and blood. I am just asking you to really take a moment and let that sink in when you're drawing the battle lines.

As I have said repeatedly, what's done is done, now you have to make it work. No matter the custody arrangement, whenever you have your kids, really pour into them all you've got. They need your love and your commitment that they can count on you to take care of them. Their home is now gone and you are living somewhere else; they will need time to adjust and feel safe in this new situation. Do what you can to help that process. Have food in the fridge, clean sheets on their bed, and pay attention to them when they are over with you; don't let them feel that they have to compete with the television and the ball game that is tied and now in overtime.

Also, don't talk to your children like they are adults and tell them the horrible situation you are in because of their mother. They don't need to hear you rail on their mom, no matter what really happened that caused the divorce. She is still their mom; do what you can to preserve that role for your ex-spouse, because it will help your children in the long run. You still need to be their dad, because you are the only dad they have; you can't check out on them. It's so important that you heal and recover so you can reassure your children that everything will be all right.

Your children's future is something you shouldn't gamble with, so choose them over anything else you might fancy. They are your legacy and they are not to be left with a neighbor when your schedule says you're free. Be the parent, be the dad and love your children through this. It will be worth the effort.

Diarrhea

This word is a real showstopper; it really gets your attention. All of us have been victimized by the onslaught of diarrhea and felt its crippling effect on our body. The causes of this plight are food poisoning and sickness. Food poisoning comes from ingesting food that was not prepared or cooked correctly or food that was not held at a correct temperature, therefore allowing bacteria to multiply and causing us to get sick. Another way to contract this illness is to be around people who have been or are now sick and are not careful enough about hygiene; you get too close and you catch the bug.

The topic I want to pursue here is people who have diarrhea of the mouth. I am talking about people who talk too much. When you're going through a divorce, it is real tempting to want to talk to anyone who will listen to you. That is a recipe for disaster, as not everyone who agrees to listen to you can be trusted with your words. Here you are pouring out your heart about every detail of what happened before, during and after your divorce, and they can't wait to run and tell the world. Let me caution you to be very careful about spewing every detail of what happened or is happening in your life. Not everybody needs to know and not everybody cares. Your life and problems are yours, and what you share is precious information, so you should screen all potential listeners. Also be very careful how you answer the questions that are asked of you. Some people are very good at baiting you into spilling your guts with very sneaky questions that lead you down a path of telling every jot and tittle of your story.

I would also be careful of listening to others who want you to listen to every detail of their life. There are a lot of folks who are just so negative that after thirty minutes with them you want to go slit your wrists. Their glass is so half empty and their life is so unfair that you just get dragged down to their miserable level of existence. It was hard enough to make it through your divorce and find a positive way back into society. Now you have to be careful to not surround yourself with or listen to negative friends or relatives. You can be kind and respectful, but don't subject yourself to that kind of talk.

Remember that you will get better with each new day; find a trusted counselor or friend to go on that journey with you. Sharing bits and pieces with people who don't have the perspective of where you have been or where you are going is dangerous, to say the least. You can be very superficial with them, your occasional concerned friends, but you can't dive deep with them about the really important details of your recovery.

So remember that diarrhea usually comes from others or from ingesting something you shouldn't, so be careful about who you associate with and who you listen to. *Your divorce may be public knowledge, but it doesn't have to be everybody's business.* I would just caution you to be careful about what you tell and whom you tell it to. You can't control others and what they say, whether they're friends or even family, but you need to be responsible for what rolls off your tongue and out of your heart.

Devastation

In the aftermath of any natural disaster we all see the devastation left behind by the wind or rain or by the earth giving us a good shake. As a nation we have spent a lot of money on early warning systems and radar to tell us when the conditions are right for the storm to manifest itself. Yet none of the systems can ever prevent the storm from coming or prevent the damage and death it leaves behind.

As in any storm, once the danger passes the residents emerge to assess the damage. In some parts of the country people open storm cellar doors to see a neighborhood that has been destroyed and in no way resembles the street on which they have lived for years. Teams of folks who were not affected stream in to lend a hand to remove debris and search for survivors. So it is in the days after your divorce: The storm has passed and you now live in a world of devastation. What you had is now gone and those you once loved are missing. If you are lucky, a few friends come to check on you and see if you are okay and assess whether you're going to make it. Like most storm victims, you are just stunned by the loss; you can't process that your years of marriage have now ended. You can't speak, you can't think…you can only exist, and at times you feel that you can't go on.

But every community that has experienced a storm rebuilds over time. The residents come to grips with the damage and begin to gather the broken pieces and put them in the trash and then grab a hammer and materials and start to put the town back together. Just as those residents rebuild their lives, you must begin to rebuild your life from this divorce. The destroyed area left by the storm will never look the same, because what was once there is now gone. New structures will now replace the old ones, and although they are erected in the same places the buildings will be new and different. As we have stated many times, you will never be the same person after the divorce as you were when you were married. The tragic reality is that some divorced folks just sit and do nothing, resembling a community that never rebuilt after the storm. They just continue to sit in the rubble and feel sorry for themselves. It's time for you to sweep away whatever debris the storm has left and start a new life and rebuild yourself.

With the help of a trusted counselor, begin to lay a foundation that you can build on. Come to grips with the fact that the new you will be different and will now trek on a different path. Once you get that deep down inside of you, you can begin to erect walls and a roof to protect you and to allow you to set up shop and continue on with life. Get excited about how you can now pick out all new stuff to go into you, just like you would design and furnish a new house. Get in touch with your passions and fill your new life with stuff that you like to do and things that make you happy. Find your fulfillment in overcoming the storm and in then being able to help other storm victims as you rebuild your own life. You can always talk about what used to be, but it helps to have perspective when you have built a new life over the one that the storm took down.

Despair

Ever watch a television commercial or program in which a foundation or group is trying to raise money for starving children? I don't know about you, but I can't watch that for very long; the despair on the faces of those hungry children is too much to bear. Can you imagine the mental anguish of a hungry child, or worse yet, the mother of those children? It's a feeling of utter helplessness. It's a maze with no way out.

Surviving a divorce is sorta like that. You still may be able to reach the fridge or make it to the local market on payday, but the feeling of utter helplessness is a constant companion. You can't breathe, you can't do anything but exist…and even that sucks the life right out of you. You don't want to see anyone, talk to anyone; you're embarrassed for anyone to see you like this, especially those who knew you as part of a once healthy marriage. You feel like a failure to yourself, and if you have any children, you now hold yourself responsible for the separated life that they now face.

Now comes the time when we have got to put some air back in that tire. The divorce and the anger and bitterness have sucked all the life out of you, and now it's time to fill up that void with a new dose of perspective. It's done, you're divorced, now let's deal with it. Life is not over, it's just different now; realizing that is the first step in your journey to a new you. You have to turn the page and start plotting out a path to recovery and restoration. The ink on the past pages has dried and is there forever, done, with no way to retrace or relive those times. Your constant replaying of the events that led up to your divorce will only fuel the despair that is now paralyzing you.

You have got to get your head turned around and start looking forward. God isn't for divorce, but He is for divorced people and will be there when you start to ask Him the question, "What now?" Down this new road you will find the new you, meaning that the person you were before the divorce no longer exists. God wants to use the divorce to forge a new creation out of the failure that was your marriage. So let's stop with the desire for everything—and by "everything" I mean you and your circumstances—to be like it once was; as I said, that is a place that no longer exists. The new work that God wants to do with you will replace that despair with hope and energy to become the new creature that God is just waiting to create.

The scripture teaches that God causes all things to work out for good for those who are called by His name and for His purpose. This promise includes your divorce and the despair that now fills your lungs. Exhale that despair and fill your lungs with hope. You will find that this exchange will set the stage for your new life.

Deserve

This word is a powder keg of emotional response because it's usually verbally launched by one or both sides in the midst of a divorce. When you say you "deserve" something, you are justifying what you have or what you want; it all depends on which end of the statement you're on.

Rarely are there divorces in which there is a peaceful agreement on every item on the list of topics that need attention and a decision. The topics range from children and time with each parent, to assets and money that need to be divided among the parties. There is leverage and manipulation around every corner with regard to getting what you want and what you don't want the other to have. That is why these proceedings can get ugly and common sense and common ground can go out the window due to the jealousy of one or both. So men, let me challenge you with a very tender topic. Please hear me out....

Your children—do you want them, or do you just want to cause your ex-spouse pain from not having her children all of the time? Do you have a place to have your children over? Do you really want your children with you? Are you really interested in spending quality time with your children, instead of sticking them in front of a television set and calling that "quality time"? If you have a place and you truly want your children, then you deserve to have them, and you should fight for that time.

Your children are not a negotiating tool or a bargaining chip; they are your flesh and blood and you are their father. If you feel that you deserve time with your children, then parent them when you have them and do not use your time with them to pump them for information about their mother. They are hurting just as you are, so you don't need to spend your time having adult conversations with your children. They don't want to hear the details of the divorce; they are living it. Spend time with them where they are, and in their struggle, help them to know that you love them and want them. That will do more to calm their hearts and give them peace and security. I would also try not to put your children in a position of having to choose between mommy and daddy; that really tears them up inside. They don't want to choose, they just want peace between you and their mom, and at least you can promise them that. You can't let your frustrations with your ex-spouse invade your time with your children. They are powerless and in the middle of all the choices you and your ex will make. Please walk a mile in their shoes; you will be better for it and you will enjoy your children more.

If you yourself came from divorced parents, then you can really echo my last few comments. It's hard for everyone involved, so don't make it more difficult by asking for things you don't deserve. Your children will gravitate to the parent who will understand them and provide love and security and wisdom. If you find your children drifting away from you, then look in the mirror and ask yourself to rethink your actions. Stop thinking that you deserve your children's love and respect just because you're their dad. You don't *deserve* their love and respect, you *earn* it.

Desert

The second chapter of Exodus starts to detail the life of Moses. Do you remember reading this in the Bible or watching it unfold on television in the movie *The Ten Commandments*? I love the part in the movie where Rameses took Moses to the edge of the desert and left him there after it was learned that Moses was indeed Hebrew. He left him there alone with a few days of food and a walking staff. Rameses told Moses to make the desert his own kingdom where he could rule over the snakes and scorpions. You know how the story ends: While Moses is in the desert he meets his wife and establishes another family and then has the encounter with God Almighty. Then after Rameses becomes Pharaoh, Moses returns with the famous words, "Let my people go!" After the numerous plagues, Pharaoh lets the Hebrew people go and they leave Egypt for the land flowing with milk and honey.

I know after my divorce I felt that I had been led to the edge of my desert and left there. I had no idea of where I was or what to do. I no longer had my home, my children, or my furniture; I left home with my clothes and my car and moved into a bedroom at my mother's house. Half of my money was gone and so was half of my retirement—gone with a judge's signature. Can you relate? Maybe you have just been handed your walking staff and had to leave the house where you raised your family. It's no fun, believe me.

It's very quiet in the desert, and the quiet after your divorce is just deafening. Whether you move in with a family member or you are lucky enough to go to an apartment, the silence is almost unbearable when you have been used to a house full of children or teens. That for me was the first unbearable thing that haunted me: the silence that I now lived in. There was no one to say, "Hey, Dad, come and help me with my homework." The worst was going to bed without the routine of praying with my children and then kissing them goodnight. I now was texting my two older children goodnight, and my youngest I could not communicate with at bedtime. I just remember many nights in tears over what I was missing and what had been taken from me. Now that is the desert and I was walking and living in it.

Just like Moses, it was in the desert where I began to get in touch with what had happened to me and learn how to survive in a foreign land. A new job came my way, and later I was able to purchase a home again and things were moving on to a new normal. Looking to God for His provision and not drowning in blame or self-pity is the key to coming through the desert alive. The desert will toughen you up and you will see and recognize more of God's little blessings as He brings you out step by step. While you may see others and your ex-spouse just living it up as if nothing had ever happened, the key is to focus on the new man that God is making you to be. Remember the law of sowing and reaping—it applies in the desert as well as in the land of plenty. Your hard work will be rewarded and you will come out twice blessed as you have let the desert refine you as pure gold. So don't mind the heat while you're in the desert, because with God, it's no sweat!

Describe

One of the most unique things about our existence is that if we are privileged with speech we have the opportunity to describe the events of our life to others. We get to try our hand at using nouns and verbs, adjectives and adverbs to tell the story of where we were or where we are going. We can also tell others how we feel and what our dreams are, and we get to use our own language to do it in. From cradle to grave our lives are full of our descriptions of our experiences as we relate them to those around us.

The Bible is full of folks describing to us things they witnessed and things they professed. From staffs that turn into serpents to pots that once poured water but now pour out new wine, we get to read about what happened told by those who were there. I just marvel at the stories and the descriptions that are used to bring stories of old to life and how they touch our hearts even today. Feeding 5,000 people from a few loaves and some fish… A storm that was hushed by two words from Jesus… What are your favorite stories of the Bible? Jonah in the belly of a great fish is a favorite of mine. Maybe you've been moved by the crucifixion of our Savior, Jesus Christ.

Just remember as you move through your divorce, watch the words that roll off of your tongue. I know it's hard when your heart is hurting and you just want to have someone to talk to but it seems that no one understands. The sad fact is that regular folks don't find much comfort with those of us who are going through a divorce. If they themselves have never been through a divorce, they shy away from us like we've got the plague. I don't think they mean to, they just don't know how to comfort us when we are hurting. That is why you should select your confidants very carefully. If you are choosing the wrong people to confide in, you will soon think that you have no one to talk to, which isn't the truth at all. It's just that you are choosing the wrong people to share your hurt with. It takes a very special person to hear the hurt of the heart and then to offer comfort to the one who is hurting. You may be choosing friends who aren't good at listening, meaning they care but have no understanding to help you, or you may be choosing good listeners but they have a tendency to run and blab your woes all over town.

I can remember the number one question that used to haunt me: "How are you doing?" I used to think that if someone asked, that meant they were interested in my answer. But just as I would get rolling on my spiel I would find them growing uneasy with me. They didn't want to hear every detail of my anguish, they were really asking for the *Reader's Digest* version. I soon wised up and started giving shorter and eventually more positive answers instead of rants of woe. I saved my exhaustive conversations for my Christian counselor, who could help me and had the time to listen and, most of all, was concerned about my recovery.

You paint your path with the words that you choose, so choose them wisely. Do you talk of bitterness and defeat, or have you turned the corner and choose to speak of forgiveness and a new direction in life? Let God come and change your trouble to triumph so you can one day have a story worth retelling.

Deploy

In every crisis in which our nation's interests are at stake or we are called on to help another country defend its borders, our military has to be ready to deploy. Webster defines *deploy* as "to spread out and present a wider front." When it's determined what's needed and when, resources are gathered and logistics personnel begin to send them into the battlefield.

As you emerge from your battlefield you may not have any logistic personnel to call on. That is why many times in this book I recommend that you find and use a professional counselor. He or she can help you analyze your situation and put you on a plan to recover and discover the new you after your divorce. Some of the re-creation will come from the counselor's suggestions, but realize that you will have the opportunity to participate in the change. Let's take a look at deployment from both angles as we talk about putting Humpty Dumpty back together again.

Your counselor will provide a sounding board for you as you both begin sifting through the events leading up to your divorce. Along with that there will be the independent study of who you are, going all the way back to your childhood to learn how you came together as a child, youth and adult. It's your God-given *DNA* that will determine what your gifts are and what and who you desire to become in the days ahead. You are now free to become all God created you to be, to break the chains of all the negative things spoken over you and to receive His forgiveness for all of your past mistakes. Receiving God's forgiveness is the key as you reestablish your connection with the Savior and now decide to follow Him. A clean slate and a desire to jump-start your life can only help you as you and your counselor chart a course of renewal and redemption. But you must receive it and not be so mired in guilt that you don't believe you deserve a second chance. Of course you don't deserve it; none of us do, but that is why we all are in need of a Savior. Grace, His unmerited favor, gets showered on those who will receive it and let it wash them clean from their checkered past.

Lastly, let's talk about what you can and need to do to help you. First, give yourself permission to change. Your divorce has happened; now let's get on with life. Stop reliving every horrible mistake and loss; what has happened will not change no matter how many times you think about it. Another fun thing you can do if your funds will allow is to go buy some new clothes. I know that might sound ridiculous, but new clothes just might help you discover the new you. And while you're at it, gather some of your old clothes and take them down to Goodwill and then say goodbye to them and to the old you. Try a new haircut or buy some new shoes, anything to get you thinking and moving forward. A new health club membership might just be the ticket to reshaping a battle-worn you. Your new positive direction will also involve some new friends: trusted, loyal, dependable friends who will deploy themselves around you and protect you as you emerge from your past into a bright future.

Delilah

FROM OUR DAYS IN SUNDAY school we have heard the story of Samson and Delilah. This is a story of romance and deceit that ended in death—how tragic. Here's a guy who had it all, the blessing of God in his life and superhuman strength, and he let a glance at a harlot and a relationship with her cost him his destiny and eventually his life.

One of the biggest mistakes that divorced men make is not taking time to heal properly. I know that I might step on some toes here, but some guys, as soon as they are free from their ex-spouse, are on the prowl seeking female companionship to replace what they just lost. Nothing could be more dangerous than signing your divorce papers and then finding yourself out with the guys looking for another relationship or a one-night stand. What's needed after your divorce is some time to yourself to rest and absorb the reality of your new status. We all know the trauma and emotions that come with parting ways with our spouse; we feel a lot of anger that sometimes spills over into hate as we part with kids, cash and a few of our toys. Sex or female companionship will only delay the healing of our wounds. I know how tempting it can be to release all the tension of your divorce on some meaningless date. If you really want a supernatural healing that only God can provide, let's take a breath and consider a few points.

Your future and destiny now lie in your hands, and the steps that you now take can make or break that outcome. What you want to replace is not lack of sex or female companionship; rather, what you need is God's love and forgiveness to be the first on the scene to start the healing process. Understanding that God isn't for divorce but He is for divorced people can really have a calming effect on you. Now you can relax and know that God is not mad at you, He is ready to take your mess and make something out of it. He has a plan for your life, and you can only know that if you are in a quiet place in your heart to hear it.

The real test here is to resist the temptation of another relationship and instead work on your relationship with the Lord. Maybe some of your friends are now trying to set you up, or hook you up with one of their female friends, but please, not yet. You need to spend time with your pastor or counselor and fix the things that need fixing with regard to your person. This is a great opportunity to repair the damage done in the course of the divorce, as you had issues that were a part of the breakup. Find out what those areas are and make a plan to become a better man than you were before the divorce.

Who do you do this for? Well, you do it for you and your children, and if God allows you to remarry one day, then you do it for her. Let's come out of this with a plan to improve and get better and get our relationship with the Lord nailed down. Lay a good foundation of hard work and get yourself ready for the exciting things that God still has for you. Becoming a better man, a better parent and a better person will all lead to a happier you in the long run. A good-looking woman picked up at a club can't do that for you, so let's not go there. Your strength, like Samson's, comes from the God of the heavens. Be careful who you share that with!

Delete

One of the most frequently hit keys on your computer keyboard is the delete key. This key removes mail, documents or your most recent keystrokes. All of those deleted items then get sent to the deleted file, and from there you empty all the trash. A failure to regularly delete items and dump your deleted file will cause your computer to run slow as it has to contend with more and more information, some needed and some worthy of dumping.

The same can be said of you after your divorce. There are some things that you just need to forget. It's common to continue to rehash the memories of what used to be and all the times you feel you should have acted differently or made a different decision. You now find yourself in an unfamiliar situation: divorced and in no-man's-land. You don't recognize a thing, and all the effort you exert won't bring your family back together. So you hit rewind on the past and start to relive it, playing the game of "What if." I know it's hard—been there and done that—but you can't change one minute of the past no matter how many times you relive it. It's time to hit the delete button and start to dump the memory files of all the hurtful past. Decide what has to go and start to forget it. All the negative things said about you and all the circumstances that played out on you that you could not control…let them go. You can't do anything about them anyway.

When God talks about forgiving our sins (Psalm 103), He uses the analogy of removing our transgressions from us as far as the east is from the west. That distance is immeasurable, and so it should be with you: start forgetting what you don't need to remember. Another thing, don't let other people keep you down by reminding you of your past failures and mistakes. Either tell them to stop or get some new friends. Don't allow anyone to speak those negative words to you or over you. You don't have to engage them in a debate or conversation about what happened; just walk away and leave it alone.

Some files you need to keep and preserve; those would be all the blessings of God in your life that you will take with you in the days ahead. You don't want to delete these; in fact, you want to save them in very safe places. Photos and journal entries are great places to store the good things that you can use to gain a fresh start. Let your counselor help you to sort through the rubble and find all the treasures that are in your memories and start rebuilding yourself.

As time moves you further from your divorce, you will feel better and see things more clearly. As you do, keep the momentum by keeping your distance from anything or anybody that would attempt to drag you back into what is now the past. A new direction and new habits and interests are the recipe for forging ahead with your new life. Everyone is different, so pay attention to how you are doing. See your counselor regularly and treasure that relationship. At this writing it's been seven years for me, and I still see Dr. Stoddard and talk about my new path.

The delete key on a keyboard is always in the same place for every user, but everyone's personal delete key is located in a unique place. Your job is to find yours and use it.

Deep

One great thing about most swimming pools is that the depth is recorded along the side of the pool as you go from the shallow to the deep end. For parents, knowing the depth of the water is crucial as you need to know which end you can safely allow your child to play in. As a child I would slide my hands along the side of the pool and with my feet shuffle down toward the deep end. There came a point in my journey when my feet would lose contact with the bottom and I knew that if I lost my grip on the side of the pool I would be in trouble. That was enough to get me to hustle back to where my feet could touch and the water level was safe.

Jesus asked the disciples in Luke 5 verse 4, "Put out into the deep water and let your nets down for a catch." Jesus knew where the fish were and He was instructing Peter on where to let down the nets, but note that Peter and the boys had been fishing all the previous night and caught nothing. I love Peter's response to the Savior, "Because you ask, I will let down the nets." And the scripture goes on to say that the nets could not contain all the fish that were caught. My point is that most of life's biggest catches lie in the deepest waters. Yet we remain coast huggers, not venturing out in the deeper waters where we can face our fears and embrace our destiny.

Our divorce sometimes forces us into running for cover or for the shallowest water we can find so we can heal and be restored from the ills of all the pain we have endured. This can take a toll on our dreams and our self-confidence, to the point that we forget that we need to pick ourselves up and get going again. After you have rested and healed from your trauma, the next steps on the road to recovery require you to get up and start walking toward your future, wading out beyond the shallows.

There is life after your divorce. To find it, you have to get in touch with who you are and what you are gifted at and get moving again. A complete inventory of your interests, along with your counselor's guidance, can help you map out a direction for you to reengage with life. I know that if you are pushing middle age, you may think you don't have many productive years left to give to anyone or to society in general, but I am here to plead with you to stop believing that lie. Your life is not over, it's really just beginning again. You have been set free, so to speak, through your divorce, not to go hide but to focus on what God has for you in your remaining years. The exciting part of your new life is that when you're ready, God is ready to guide you into deeper waters where, just like Peter experienced, your nets cannot contain all the fish that are there for the catching.

Overcome your fears, and stop listening to those around you who constantly remind you of your past and try to keep you from moving on. Let's get going and leave the safe shallow waters for the deep. You might need to find a trusted friend or pastor to hold your hand as you feel the waters begin to rise as you walk toward your goals. Trust that He is a faithful God and, as the scripture also says, that He will never leave you or forsake you. Remember, when you're in over your head, it doesn't matter how deep the water is. You reap when you're in deep.

Dedicate

I remember the first time I heard the word *dedicate*. It was at a dance in junior high. The buzz at the dance was that the DJ was allowing students to grab the mic and dedicate a song to their date. Sorry to say, I was puzzled at why this was such a big deal. Not knowing the meaning of the word, I was just lost for a moment. Webster says that when you dedicate something it's like you honor them with whatever you are dedicating. So back to the dance… When I found out that I could dedicate a song to my date, it was like the Bee Gees were singing my favorite song to her and the words they were singing were coming straight from me. How cool that the Bee Gees could help me make points at the dance—it worked!

No doubt you have lost that junior high feeling as you deal with your divorce; the thought that this relationship has gone south is such a downer. There is nothing quite like a divorce to suck the life right out of you and leave you paralyzed. I can remember days and weeks of just having a glazed look on my face, without expression, just plain lost. "Where do I go from here?" and "What will I do?" are just two of the many questions I'm sure you can relate to. At some point in this process the light bulb will go on and you will find the gear that will start your climb back into society. That gear is what I want to visit with you about.

Exodus 32 verse 29 says, "Then Moses said, 'Dedicate yourselves today to the Lord.'" This plea comes after the children of Israel had fallen into sin while Moses was up on the mountain receiving the Ten Commandments. No doubt you played a part in your divorce. I am not asking for a confessional here, but what I am asking is for you to recognize your part. I don't really care what you did or what she did; the fact remains that you were part of it, and you share a portion of the blame for the demise of the marriage. Now that we have that settled, let's go on to the next and most important step: your recovery. Accept God's forgiveness, forgive yourself for your actions, forgive her, and move on. This may take some time to work its way through your system, but until you learn to forgive you will be stuck in the blame game, always mulling over in your mind those instant replays of an incident or two that you can point to and point a finger at. You gotta let that kind of stuff go. It's futile and really serves no purpose other than to keep you stuck in your recovery.

My plea is for you to dedicate yourself to getting better through some good counseling and learning and practicing forgiveness. God still has a wonderful plan for your life, it's just now going in a different direction and will have a different ending. Philippians 3:13 says that we should forget what lies behind us and reach forward to what lies ahead. Verse 14 tells us to press on toward the goal of knowing the call of God in our life. Don't stay stuck in what happened; it was a heartbreaker for sure, but your life is calling for you to get up and get familiar with what God has for you down this new road. So you crashed your bicycle... It's time to right yourself and get back on it. Sure you've got some scratches that will scar, but keep pedaling: there are great things just down the new road. Honor yourself with your newfound dedication that you will pick up the pieces and forge ahead and leave what happened in the past, where it happened and where it belongs.

Death

I CAN REMEMBER AS IF IT were yesterday, the night my father died. My mom and sisters were standing at his bedside as the end of his life drew to a close. As death came for him, his breathing became slower and less rhythmic than normal. The deep breaths were not expelled as readily, and after each exhale, there was a pause before the next breath was drawn. This pace started to slow and then I started anticipating the last time fresh oxygen would fill his lungs. Moments later the last breath came. I watched my father's chest rise with a huge inhale, and then the exhale, and then silence. I watched and hoped that he would grab just one more breath, but that breath never came. That was it. His life ended and I was confronted with a circumstance I had never known: fatherlessness. My father was gone from this earth forever and I would never see him alive again in this life. Over the next few days I had many opportunities to view his body, but the days of seeing him alive had ended that night in the hospital.

That is the extreme difference between death and divorce. Your marriage has died and is gone forever, yet in most circumstances your ex-spouse is still alive. I know that all of our experiences are different, meaning that some of you just downright hate your ex, while others have cultivated a peaceful and workable relationship with her. But in reality the pain never goes away and we are reminded about the tremendous loss we all feel because of our divorce. Every time we have to deal with issues with our ex, whether it is about children, child support, behavior or what have you, the interaction can be very taxing. As your lives go in different directions there is an inevitability that causes friction. That is the hard thing that I am trying to convey here: The divorce ended the life of my marriage, yet in a sense it hasn't ended. The lingering dealings with my ex keep me involved and daily or weekly I am confronted with the decaying remains of my marriage.

The only coaching I would give you is to make the best of it. If you're still dealing with feelings of hate and blame, I would ask you to make peace with all of it. The fact that you are going to have to deal with your ex-wife until one of you passes gives you cause to accept that she is going to be a part of your life until one life is over, yours or hers. Everyone around you, especially your children, will benefit from a civil tone from you. Take the high road, even if she refuses to reciprocate with a mature tone. I am not telling you to lie down and let her run all over you. In some cases you need to stand your ground and fight for what is right. But what I am saying is that if you have to deal with your ex, make the best of it and get along. You don't have to like the direction of her life or her decisions, but when you have to interact, especially where the children are concerned, at least try. I know that some of you have extreme cases where it's not good and it's a battle every time you interact with your ex; all I can say to you is to ask God for His wisdom.

Part of moving forward after your divorce is learning how to deal with a life and a death at the same time.

Deal

Growing up I loved to watch the TV game show *Let's Make a Deal.* The famous host, Monty Hall, was the ultimate deal maker. Just as the contestant was certain of a prize, Monty would increase the risk at a chance at another prize of greater value. If they made the wrong decision they could lose what they had, but if they made the right choice they could walk away with a greater prize. It was nerve-racking as Monty always found a way to make every decision a difficult one. Another exciting part of the show came when a contestant had to choose one of three doors, each door with something hidden behind it. Prizes like cars and boats and kitchen appliances might be tucked away behind one of those doors, but everyone also knew that one door concealed a gag prize. The contestant could end the game ecstatically happy or completely deflated, depending on which door they chose.

Your divorce is no game show, but you could call it *Let's Make a Deal*, if you play your cards right. Hardly ever does either party have all of their demands met by the other side. The key is to go into your negotiations with an idea of what you want and what you need. The details of your divorce move at different speeds, with regard to the courts and the back-and-forth between the two attorneys. If communication between you and your ex has totally broken down, you can spend thousands of dollars discussing everything under the sun with letters generated from the lawyers. These issues can drag out for months, or as long as the one doing the dragging can pay their attorney fees.

My advice here is to do your best to compromise where you can and play hardball where it matters most. Some people have a motive behind dragging matters on for months: they want to weaken the other side into making concessions they would never have agreed to otherwise. If you are arguing over things, let them go if you can; you can always replace your stuff. But if it's your children you're arguing about, it might take some time to negotiate a parenting plan that you can live with. This is not a winner-take-all type of contest as some would argue; you have to decide what's important and give ground on less precious areas.

Consider what's most important to you in this deal. I would be careful about letting the other side know what those things are, as they might hold them as bargaining chips to gain concessions in other areas. I know from experience, I didn't want to fight, I just wanted the whole process over and done with, but I had to let my attorney carry my concerns to the other side.

Try not to make your negotiations about the emotional pain you feel, but rather what is right and what you deserve. If you choose the emotional battle, you might find anger and spite driving your decisions instead of fairness and doing the right thing. Do your best to remain calm and trust God to fight your battles for you. Choose an attorney who will fight for you and at the same time truly represent your wishes and conduct them accordingly. Try to keep negotiation from getting ugly; make peace and concessions where you can. Fight for what is right and what you deserve and make sure that you have a good parenting plan that is fair.

The judge won't be Monty Hall, nor will there be doors to choose from. It's going to take a calm heart and a clear mind to make this deal.

DEAF

HAVE YOU EVER THOUGHT ABOUT the five senses of the human body? Sight, hearing, touch, taste and smell all come together to give you a chance to take in all that is happening in your life. We have all encountered others who, either from birth or through an accident, are missing one or more of their senses. In most cases the remaining senses become enhanced to make up for whatever is missing, sometimes producing spectacular results.

Going through my divorce was like being in a meat grinder; I felt physically and emotionally wiped out. You can even feel like a few of your senses have been overloaded and some just want to shut down. Or you might feel like other people's senses aren't working. You have spent time on the witness stand in court, and everything you have said now comes back to you all twisted and hardly resembling what you originally said. Did they really hear you? Or maybe you're just tired of all the yelling and hearing the painful cries of your children as they are forced to live their lives out of a suitcase.

Those kinds of stresses can cause anyone to want to shut down or just tune out and stop listening as intently as you used to. Maybe you describe it as just being numb and you stop feeling as deeply or caring like you used to. Whatever it is that is shutting down in you, just know that it's still there, you may just need a little time to help with your perspective on life.

I know from my own experience I can really relate to the examples I just described. I hated to look into the eyes of my children and see the hurt that was exploding from their facial expression. I remember trying to take coaching or counsel from my pastor and then feeling like I was running in a slow-motion movie, unable to react and make the changes necessary. I had a hard time talking to my children and explaining to them why and how this divorce came to be and how it really rocked their world.

I remember one night my kids and I were going to watch a movie, *Mrs. Doubtfire* with Robin Williams. When that movie first came out I really liked it, I really thought it was funny, and on this night with my kids I thought it would be a fun thing to watch. I had totally forgotten the movie is about divorced parents and how Robin Williams would do anything to have time with his children, even to the point of dressing up as an old lady to get hired to babysit his own children. Somehow, after my own experience with divorce, that movie isn't funny to me anymore. That night we picked out a different movie.

Just remember, you came through a divorce and now you have to figure out how to move beyond that in a positive manner. Life just changed, and you need to change with it and be there for your children as they will be looking to you for answers as to how you are all going to get through this. You are going to need all the senses God handed out to you to get that done with them and yourself. I know you may still be hurting and wondering if you can recover. Let me tell you that you can! Do the hard work, get some good counsel and work on getting your senses firing on all cylinders. God has now given you a ministry opportunity to help other divorced folks and speak to the children of divorce. One day you will have that chance to encourage another divorced person with what you have learned, I can sense it.

Dawn

At dawn, the sun makes its grand appearance on the horizon and announces to the earth that it's time to start a new day. As sunrise appears, the night's darkness begins to slip away and the light of the new day starts to illuminate the eastern sky. The sky continues to brighten as the sun nears the point where the sky touches the earth…and then at the magic moment the sun shows itself and the day begins.

Well, for the divorced guy the dawn of a new day can be either good news or bad news. For me the beginning of each new day was dreaded. The only comfort I could find was the nighttime, when I could sleep and escape the challenge of living another day. The morning meant that I had to go face a public I was not ready to face. I felt like everyone knew every horrible detail of my recent divorce and I was not ready to function as a single man/dad yet. Of course that was a huge exaggeration I had let build up in my mind, and it's that kind of thinking that kept me from getting better quicker. Your ability to recover will always be determined by who you are listening to. If it's you and your counselor, then you stand a better chance than if you're listening only to yourself or another divorced friend who has not allowed himself to overcome his own bad thinking.

A friend of mine had a different experience: He loved the dawn of a new day but hated the night. He hated the darkness and being alone in his bed trying to go to sleep. For him the dawn couldn't come soon enough as he had a hard time sleeping and turning off his brain so sleep could come. There is something to be said about a good night's sleep, but when you can't find peace of mind and night after night you replay every horrible moment of your past and then think of a future alone, it is no wonder you can't sleep. The worst thing is that you feel you need to medicate yourself to sleep. Be careful of that slippery slope. As I have said many times, a peace of mind will come when you begin to heal your mind with counseling. Sleeping pills might make you feel drowsy so you can sleep, but they can't bring peace to your conflicts.

The dawn that we need to focus on is the dawn of the new you. Say goodbye to the past of what happened and the mistakes that contributed to you being where you are. You had a hand in it, so own that part of it, but now let's move on. The dawn of the new you will now start to be focused on how you are going to live your life as a divorced, single man who still has dreams and a future. You have to see yourself as a bright shining star, not a dull, worthless individual who has lost everything. You may have suffered some losses, but your attitude of how you see yourself will allow that new person to emerge, if that attitude is positive. Get yourself surrounded by friends and family who are committed to you and stop hanging around negative people who love to talk about how rough their life is. We all have had bad things happen; that is not the problem. The real issue is, will you meet the sun every morning and live the rest of your life excited about all the possibilities each new day has to offer?

DAVID

I LOVE THE STORY OF DAVID and Goliath in the seventeenth chapter of 1 Samuel. It captures the very essence of someone having a different opinion than everyone else and doing something about it. At the time of this story, Israel was battling the Philistines and the young man David, not yet old enough to be in the army, was out tending his father's flock of sheep. One day David was asked by his father to take some food up to the front lines of the battle to give to his brothers. The battle was at a standstill, as a giant was taunting the army of God. Goliath stood nine feet nine inches, his armor alone weighed 125 pounds, and just the tip of his spear weighed sixteen pounds. A big dude!

The deal that Goliath was trying strike with the army of Israel was a winner-take-all duel. Instead of the armies clashing and having lots of blood spilt, Goliath offered to fight a one-on-one duel with whichever warrior of Israel would come forward. The loser's army would become the servants of the victor. The taunting went on for days, for as soon as Goliath would come to the front line to face a challenger, no one would step forward to fight him, because they were too scared to fight.

Upon arriving at the camp, David witnessed the giant and his daily taunt of the army of Israel and was in disbelief that no one had the guts to step forward and face the giant. David got in front of King Saul and requested that Saul give him permission to fight the giant. In verse 33, Saul says, “You are but a youth; he has been a warrior since his youth.” David responds that as a shepherd he has killed lions and bears while protecting his flocks; this giant is nothing in his eyes. Saul granted David his wish and offered him some armor for the battle, but David refused the armor and just took what he had used to fight as a shepherd: five smooth stones from the brook and his sling. David then ran toward Goliath and hurled one stone with his sling. The stone landed in the forehead of Goliath and the giant fell to the ground. David then took Goliath’s own sword and cut off his head.

What does this story have to do with you, one might ask? Your success in this season of going through your divorce will be linked to how you think and how you perceive the situation you find yourself in. You can either run from your battles or face them; it’s your choice. What is taunting you at the moment? Is it an attorney, your ex, or just the whole process in general? Just like the story, if you don’t fight you will be a slave to the situation and powerless until you change your mind and decide for yourself that you can fight and win.

It’s not really so much in the winning as it is in fighting for what is right. Your children, your funds and your possessions are all worth your best effort to keep them on your side of the ledger. You have too much invested in the marriage that once was to now leave empty-handed. Consider all of the years that you contributed to the family and the estate. You just need a fair shake in the deal. The giant will be as big as you make it out to be in your own mind. Invite God to fight your battles for you and together you can try to bring fairness to the process, if others will allow that to happen. If you have to dig in and fight, then that is what you have to do. It's not about *who's* right, it's about *what's* right. Just remember that as you face your giants, and just like David, your fight could be over before you know it.

Dark

WHAT IS IT ABOUT THE dark that makes most kids afraid to go to bed at night? I know while I was at home with my children, night-lights were burning strong in an electric outlet nearby. Even with the night-light burning my kids would still call down the hall for me to come running and shut the closet door to make sure a monster didn't come barreling out to get them. There is something about the dark that strikes a little fear in all of us. Have you ever been in the forest with no moon above? Now that is dark; you can't even see your hand in front of your face.

As I have visited with folks who have tasted divorce, the one word that inevitably comes rolling out of their mouth to describe the days around the time the papers were signed is *dark*. Dark is the absence of light, and it takes no amount of brilliance to know the difference between the two. When you think of the light, you think of everything seen and out in the open. In the light you can see your surroundings and navigate through them.

Contrast that with darkness. In the dark you can't see a blooming thing and you have to feel your way around like a blind person so you don't hurt yourself or stub your toe. Things happen faster in the light because of the ease of mobility, but moving in the dark is a slow, difficult process because you can't see where you're going. I am sure that as you read the last few sentences you were reliving your own experiences of wandering in the dark during your divorce. Dark days are filled with hidden obstacles that cause you pain, with no clear path out of the mess. Let me challenge you with your darkness with the next paragraph.

There are some pretty special things that happen in the dark. Deep in the earth, it's the dark places where pressures create beautiful diamonds. The formation and creation happens in a very dark place, and when a diamond is mined and then cut and fashioned, the light does its magic on the stone. Another creation that happens in a deep dark place is the moment of conception, when the egg and the sperm unite to create life. When these two powerful ingredients are joined, the power of God's creation takes place. Cells divide and organs and bone are formed. Brain tissue forms and blood vessels start carrying blood from a beating heart. So the next time you are tempted to curse the darkness you may be in at the moment, I would challenge you to ask God to create something beautiful with you while you are in your darkness. The pressure that creates the diamond may not be very pleasant, but it is necessary to produce the final product. The new life that grows in the womb goes through nine months of change that is uncomfortable for the mother, but when the child is born all the discomfort is forgotten.

So let's give the darkness a second look and turn our gaze in a different direction. You may reside in a dark place now, but just know that if you hunker down and do the hard work of transformation, God will create something beautiful when you emerge one day. Psalm 139 says in verses 11 and 12, "If I say, surely the darkness will overwhelm me and the light around me will be night, even the darkness is not dark to Thee, and the night is as bright as the day. Darkness and light are alike to Thee."

Take comfort in knowing that your darkness is only what you see. God sees it all and you are still in the palm of His hand no matter where you are in life. You can't spend your life chasing the sunset; the day is over and the light is fading and soon it will be night. Rather, if it's already dark, turn into the darkness and run toward it. Your sunrise lies just beyond the darkest part of the night, and there you can start over and begin your new day and new life.

Here is a blank page for you to capture those life changing thoughts from the pages you have just read...

Part Two

Post–Divorce, Forgiveness and Hope Are Your Keys for Your New Life

Divine Intervention

You never know how and when God will choose to show up and let you know that He is there. Some of us are so bitter and entrenched in hate that we wouldn't know God if He walked in the front door. I truly understand the mindset you may have as you walk through this most difficult time and the gut-wrenching emotions of your loss. It's easy to become isolated, to think that no one knows your struggle and no one cares or can even begin to comfort you.

The fourth chapter of John tells the story of Jesus and the woman at the well. Maybe you have read this most fascinating story where Jesus addresses this woman. In the conversation Jesus tells the woman some truths about her that shock her, because "How could this man know this about me?" In verse 29 she goes and tells her friends, "Come see a man who told me all things that I ever did." She was amazed that even with her long list of sins and the current state of her affairs, Jesus was still offering her Living Water and salvation.

Memo to self here: "God knows" and is willing to step in and help you in your hour of need. You have got to lose the mentality that you will go this alone and somehow get through it. Many do choose that strategy and find their journey long and fruitless, meaning they learn nothing and waste precious time when healing is only a prayer away. Asking God for help is not a "sissy" way out of your despair; I would argue it's the most masculine thing you can do to get the help you need. God does answer prayer, and He will hear you if you ask in faith, believing that He is and trusting Him to come to your rescue.

My story of answered prayer happened in Gallup, New Mexico. Long story short, I was calling on a customer that just happened to be the Little Sisters of the Poor. I received a phone call saying they were unhappy with a service issue and I needed to pay them a visit and fix it. I was greeted by Sister Pauline, who at six foot something was the tallest nun I had ever seen. I began to ask her about the service issue, which she was not even interested in. I was so confused by her insisting that I tell her about me, as she continued to ask, "Lynn Blackwood, why don't you tell me what's going on with you?" I had never met Sister Pauline, and I dodged her attempts for a few minutes before I just broke down in tears. At that she said, "I knew it. Why don't you tell me about what you're going through?" She had no way of knowing that those months before, I had signed my divorce papers and I was dying inside. These were the first tears I had shared with anyone publicly, and then Sister Pauline began to console me and dry my tears with her encouragement and love.

I am not even Catholic, and in my time of need God sent me a nun—now don't tell me that God doesn't know and have a sense of humor. It was so out of the blue and she was so dialed into me that there was no mistaking that meeting for anything other than Divine Intervention. God knows and is waiting for you to come to the end of yourself so He has something to work with. Ask Him today to come to your rescue and lift you into His arms and experience His love and forgiveness. Your answer may not come in the form of a nun, but rest assured that your intervention will be Divine!

Donut

Nothing can bring a dieter to their knees quicker than a warm, fresh donut. I remember when I tasted my first Krispy Kreme donut, I was hooked. Now that I have gotten older, I have to watch my consumption of these critters, because if you eat too many of them you tend to take on the shape of the donut itself. Do you know why there is a hole in the middle? I had to look this one up, but it has to do with the cooking of the donut. If you don't remove the dough from the center, the donut will not cook through enough in the hot oil, leaving the center still soft and doughy. So someone thought of removing the center so the donut could cook all the way through, thus the shape we see today.

In Matthew 6:25, Jesus talks about us being anxious for the things we need in this life, like food, clothing and shelter. He then calls our attention to the birds of the air and the lilies of the field and points out how God takes care of both. In verses 32–34, Jesus says, "Your heavenly Father knows that you need all these things. But seek first His Kingdom and His righteousness; and all these things shall be added to you. Therefore don't be anxious for tomorrow; for tomorrow will care for itself. Each day has enough trouble of its own."

What Jesus is talking about is the center of the donut. The donut can survive and actually improves without its center, but without your center you can't survive. After a divorce our head is spinning and we are so stressed, trying to make all these life-changing decisions and yet maintain our composure in public and at our jobs. We for the most part start looking like a donut: our center is missing and we are struggling to survive. We put on a good front with those around us, especially with our ex, as we don't want them to know how devastated we really are.

Jesus is saying that He knows everything you're going through, it's not a surprise to Him. So if He knows all that you're going through, you can trust Him to help you through your storm. He is asking you to seek Him first above all of your concerns. That means that you seek Him despite your financial and divorce decree concerns. His promise is that as you seek Him, all these things shall be added unto you. While others around you are jockeying for position and scheming to get over on you, you need to rest and trust that God is watching and will provide for you. Remember He feeds the birds of the air; they don't have to plant and harvest their own seed, and He feeds them. The lilies don't toil or spin, they just grow, and God adorns them with all their color and beauty. So you are just challenged to love and pursue the Savoir with all of your heart and soul. Leave the fighting and nitpicking to those who love that and the drama they stir up. Trust and obey, as the old hymn goes, for there is no other way to be happy in Jesus, than to trust and obey.

The next time you are tempted to get frustrated about your circumstances, go have a donut and remember it's what is missing in the donut that counts most with you. Your center needs to be full and connected to Jesus and tied down to the Rock of your salvation. Go ahead, have a donut; it will do you some good. It may just save your center.

DECIDE

IN THE NEW TESTAMENT THERE is a story of Jesus walking on the water one night to join His disciples in a boat (Matt 14:21-33). As Jesus came near the boat the disciples became frightened because they thought Him to be a ghost. Jesus said to them, "Take courage, it is I, don't be afraid." Then a very great thing happened. Peter asked Jesus, "If it's truly you, command me to come to YOU on the water." And Jesus said, "Come!" The scripture then says that Peter got out of the boat and walked on the water and came toward Jesus. But seeing the wind and the waves he became afraid and then started to sink and cried out, "Lord, save me!" And immediately Jesus stretched out His hand and took hold of Peter and they both got in the boat.

Now you may be asking how this story is going to help you with your divorce recovery. Plenty, I would tell you. Let me explain. Divorce is a scary thing. I'm sure you can agree that many times you have been scared about what is happening to you and how out of control things are around you. So you can identify with the disciples who were being tossed by the waves and then saw a man coming to them walking on the water: they were scared. How you process your fear is an important part of how you let what you're scared of control you. Most of the things we fear are in our mind and have little to do with the actual events in our lives; we just freak out because these things have never happened to us before. I find great comfort in the fact that Jesus said to them, "Don't be afraid, I am here." If Jesus can walk on the water and then calm the waves, surely He can handle your circumstance, no matter how scary it seems to you. I would invite you to investigate His promises and put your faith in Him.

The next part I want to address is Peter. What courage to ask Jesus to tell him to come to Him and let him walk on the water. How impossible is that kind of request? You can just hear the other eleven disciples in the boat telling Peter, "You can't do that. You're crazy. You're going to look like a real fool when you step out of the boat and disappear into the waves." But Peter kept his eyes on Jesus and turned a deaf ear to the eleven and stepped out of the boat and walked on the water. How cool is that, to actually walk on the water and prove the boys in the boat wrong! Peter had an experience where his faith overcame his fear and allowed him to do something that the others said couldn't be done. Imagine that!

There are always going to be boat people in your life. Your job is to step out of life's boat and walk away from them and not listen to them. They will keep you from the great things that God wants to do in your new life. Those boat people will always tell you every reason you can't, when the promise that is in you tells you that you can. And just know that sometimes we all have to do things when we are scared. Being scared is no reason not to do the very thing you know must be done for you to step out in faith and grow into the new you. You may never walk on water, but promise me that you will step out of the boat and do whatever it takes to establish your new identity after your divorce. Jesus is saying to you, "Come!" Now get going and don't look back.

Departure

If you've ever flown anywhere, no doubt one of the first things you did when you arrived at the airport was gaze up at the monitor looking for your flight and checking its status. So many destinations and departure times…no wonder an airport can be a frustrating place when delays hit the schedule. Weather plays a major factor in keeping customers on time, no matter the season. Another key is the status of the planes themselves: are they ready to fly? Many a flight has been cancelled due to a mechanical failure that reared its ugly head just moments before departure.

I am sure you feel that your divorce has set you back in the timetable for your life. Some of us never saw the breakup coming while others had time to brace for impact. I can relate with the airplanes that are grounded on the tarmac. They are just not ready to fly, and neither was I after things went south. It's easy to spot the grounded planes. They are towed to a safe place out of the way of the planes that are able to fly. From the outside, these planes look like they could fly, but some internal mechanical part has them parked. You may think that you can fly with those around you, but you know deep down inside that you need some work to actually get yourself off the ground. It's hard when you see others coming and going all around you and you just feel stuck. The planes that are grounded may indeed be able to get in the air, but can they fly the distance needed, and is it safe for the passengers? That's up to the mechanics to decide. It was hard to watch my personal "mechanics" pry open my compartment doors and peek inside and then detail the areas in my life that needed fixing, but I will ever be grateful to those who grounded me and helped me learn to fly again.

Divorce is not kind to your internal components. There are times after divorce when our sense of direction is severely damaged. It is an uneasy feeling not knowing whether you're coming or going or what is up or down. Besides the direction thing, you just don't feel right, meaning you are at a place in life that you just don't recognize. After ten, twenty, or more years of being married and having a routine that was working for the most part, now you find yourself alone and living an existence that is new and unsure. There is nothing more unsettling than feeling lost or uncomfortable in your own skin. You spend all of your time trying to figure out how long this will last so you can get on with being you. As I have stated many times in this book, you won't be the same, so when you look for that familiar safe place inside of yourself, it's very misleading, because it doesn't exist anymore. It's not that you will never get that sense of safety back; it's just that it will be in a different place, in a different you.

Allow God to come in and do what is necessary to get you up and flying again. It will no doubt be a bit painful and take some time, because you have undergone a major life change. Your divorce has thrown you off course and delayed your plans. It's critical that you spend some time in the shop. While you're in there, let's just go through everything and make sure that you are shipshape and ready for your departure time. You will be surprised at your new destination. Just know that your downtime is linked to the places God wants to take you to. So if it's taking a long time to prepare for departure, understand that your new destination must be worth the wait.

Deposit

Not many of us take our paycheck to the bank anymore to deposit it. Nowadays with everything being electronic, we just have our check deposited automatically. I think in a way this electronic society has jaded us into an automatic way of life. In all aspects of life we just click and solve most problems, losing the interaction skills we need to deal with real people. It's a given that your divorce has left its mark on you, but you need to not stay in that place where you feel down and defeated. The key to your survival and moving on depends on leaving that defeated mindset and walking in a more positive direction. Let's take a few metaphors from the banking world to evaluate our ability to live a positive and impactful life.

A deposit at the bank means that you actually put money in the bank; you need to have real currency and it has to slip from your hands to the teller's hand—a transaction, if you will. You can at any time make a withdrawal and take out the money you had once deposited. What the bank will not allow you to do is to take more money out than you previously put in. You may have overdraft protection, but nonetheless, your business at the bank will come to a standstill if you have a negative balance. You must have a positive balance to be a customer in good standing at the bank. Otherwise, until you make another deposit to bring your account positive, you will lose your right to bank with them. A key at the bank is to know your balance, which you can check online with a click of a mouse, or you can do it "old school" and reconcile your statement at the end of each month. Regardless of your style, your balance is critical to maintaining your banking privileges.

You're dealing with divorce now because someone made multiple withdrawals and few deposits in your marriage. Maybe the blame lies with both you and your ex-spouse, but I am concerned with you at the moment. The love in your marriage account became overdrawn, and no one checked on the balance very regularly. The manner in which you maintained your balance didn't work and the love bank shut you down. The whole issue of making more withdrawals than deposits pertains not only to your mistake, but also to allowing others to do that to you! You need to have a banker mentality: guard your accounts and do not allow yourself or anyone else to maintain a negative balance. Do you know how to reconcile a bank statement? The same practice is a skill that you need to take with you now as you move from your divorce to new relationships. Take a look at your deposits and your withdrawals. Which is the greater amount? If you care about keeping friends and family you need to learn how to keep the relationship positive. Don't allow others to practice sloppy friendships with you; hold them accountable or shut it down.

You need to manage your relationship accounts and keep positive balances for life to work. If you make a habit of taking more than you give, you will continue to be overdrawn with those you care about. Care about your balances with others. That is advice you can bank on.

DESTINY

MY FAVORITE MOVIE IS *FORREST Gump*, and I love the question Forrest asks his mom while she is on her deathbed: "Mama…what's my destiny?" She is so loving with him and then utters the most famous line of the movie: "Life is like a box of chocolates. You never know what you're going to get."

When you read chapters 37 through 50 of the book of Genesis you get a grandstand view of the life of Joseph. In thirteen chapters you see him go from son, brother and dreamer, to slave, prisoner, then to prince. You think you have had it bad with your separation and then your divorce, not to mention all the people who have let you down along the way. Well, take a moment to think about the life of Joseph. He was sold into slavery by his very own brothers who then went home and told the father that Joseph had been killed by wild animals. Then while he was a slave in the house of Potiphar, Joseph was asked by Potiphar's wife to come in and sleep with her. After he said no she grabbed him by the robe to insist that he lie with her. At that, Joseph spun out of his robe and left the room to get away from her so as not to dishonor his master, Potiphar. As the master's wife stood there in her anger she started yelling and accusing Joseph of rape. Well, that landed Joseph in prison unfairly and there he sat, innocent of the charges. All along, through each betrayal, the scripture says that the Lord was with him.

Now while in prison Joseph gained the reputation of being able to interpret dreams. Long story short, he went in front of the Pharaoh to interpret one of his dreams. During the discussion Joseph foretold seven years of prosperity and then seven years of famine, and with that wisdom Joseph was made second in command of all of Egypt. While a prince, he got a chance to see his brothers again as the seven years of famine began. With that encounter you see Joseph forgive his brothers and restore them through forgiveness.

Compared with all that Joseph went through, I don't think any of us have anything to complain about. All of our betrayals could never come close to what Joseph had to deal with. For God to use you, it's imperative that you free yourself up from bitterness and an unforgiving heart. Forgive and move on and let God give you a fresh vision of what He has for you. Make it a point to give life your very best now and set out in a new direction, where you can now allow God to direct your life. Life is full of detours, losses and setbacks, but through it all you have to dig your heels in and not give up, no matter what comes against you.

Put your faith in God and not in people. It's the approval of God that you desire, not the pat on the back from your fickle friends. God loves you so much and will bring you through this divorce no matter the circumstances and the cards you have been dealt. You must not hold on to the past as though it is something you can relive and somehow have a different outcome. What's done is done. It's time to ask God what your destiny is. I think His answer will be more fulfilling than a box of chocolates.

Dig

Most of the world's major cities have a great downtown area, where the tall buildings reside in all of their glory. Higher and higher they extend above the streets below, earning the nickname skyscrapers. If you have ever witnessed the beginning construction phases of one of these tall buildings, you'll know that you have to dig down before you ever start to build up. In fact, the depth of the hole dug is in direct proportion to the height of the building designed by its architect.

In the sixth chapter of Luke, Jesus describes a follower of His in verse 48. Jesus says, "He is like a man building a house, which dug deep and laid a foundation upon the rock; and when a flood rose, the torrent burst against that house and could not shake it, because it had been built well." In construction the least glamorous part of the project is the digging of the hole to reach the bedrock so the foundation can be poured. In fact, with most large projects a fence surrounds the construction zone and hides most of the digging, so to most of us passersby it looks like nothing is really going on. Behind the fence the shovels and big scoops are removing dirt, silt and rocks until the bedrock is reached. If the crew grows weary of digging and stops before reaching the bedrock, the stability of the building could be in jeopardy.

After your divorce, digging a new foundation may be the last thing on your mind. You want to give the appearance that you are okay and all will be well, instead of doing a little hard work first. We want to erect the walls first and get the building up because as men the last thing we want to show the world is our weakness. The real test for you is to desire to get fixed what's broken, and the key is for you to start digging. Digging in the scripture, digging in a counseling session, digging some more with your children… all with the goal of reaching your bedrock. Your bedrock may be what some call the bottom, but wherever that place is, make sure it's a place you can start to build from.

As you dig, rest assured that not many will see your efforts to reach your bedrock, so it's to your advantage not to advertise your activity. This digging is between you and God and really no one's business anyway, so just keep digging. It's hard and tough going for sure, but the one thing you're setting yourself up for is the days when your hard work begins to show. Just like a building that comes rocketing out of the ground, so will you once your foundation has been reached and poured. So how high do you want to build? After you answer that question you can determine how deep you need to dig.

It's you and God, now that you have signed your divorce papers. You owe this new life now to your children and to yourself. In this life we don't get do-overs, we just get to do things better as we move forward. Grab a good pair of gloves and a sharp shovel and let's get to work removing the dirt and rocks and dig until you hit the bedrock. There you will find the solid ground that will help your new life become resilient to life's storms.

Diary

I remember a craze from my younger years, that of keeping a diary. Most diaries sold in stores had a lock on the front and a key so you could keep your secrets hidden from your friends or parents. As with most fads, this one faded; now we call it journaling. This is a practice that I follow. I don't journal every day, but I have found it to be a great source of relief as I can get my thoughts down on paper and clear my head every once in a while.

Did you know that God has a journal? Well, that is what I like to call it. Look at Psalm 139, starting in verse 16. The psalmist says, "And in Thy book they were all written, the days that were ordained for me, when as yet there was not one of them." All of your days are already written out for you, even before you have lived them. So what you're going through is no surprise to God. Trust me, He already knows, and with that knowledge He loves you very much. Verse 17 goes on to say, "How precious also are Thy thoughts to me, O God! How vast the sum of them! If I should count them they would outnumber the sand on the seashore." Wow, God thinks about you all the time and really so many times that you can't keep track of the times His thoughts turn toward you.

My point is that you are not alone in this process of divorce and it's better to take Him along for your journey. I don't know why He has allowed this divorce to enter your life; I wonder about that same question in my own life. But it happened and now our job is to deal with it and figure out what He has for us on the other side of the separation. That is why I want you to consider keeping a journal. You need to write down your thoughts. No matter what spills out of your pen…write it down. Then as you put a little distance between you and your divorce you can easily see the progress you have made. I can remember the early days and the things I wrote down, and then as I met with my counselor I could easily open my journal and discuss with him the things that were on my heart. You will see your thoughts begin to change, and through the weeks and months you will see yourself write about different topics as you start to move forward in a positive direction.

You may not feel much like writing your thoughts down on paper, and I can certainly understand your reply, but may I still encourage you to try? The next time you are at the store, pick up a spiral-bound notebook and leave it by your bed with a pen close by. You may find it easy to start with just a few thoughts that work into a paragraph or two. Whatever rhythm suits you, I hope you find that having your thoughts down on paper will free your mind to accept new thoughts and positive ideas about your new life and direction. Some of what you have read in this book grew out of ideas and thoughts that came from nights of unrest and me just capturing my thoughts on paper. This is a good way to become reacquainted with you and come to terms with your plight and new direction. Your journal can be the key that opens up your broken heart and accelerates your recovery and healing.

Dirt

I AM A GARDEN FREAK: LOVE my flowers and rose bushes. I spend lots of time in the early spring getting the flower beds ready and waiting for the best time to plant. It takes a lot of energy to plant and then to keep the weeds from overtaking all of my pretty flowers. The benefit I get from my efforts is a beautiful lawn and flower beds and tons of compliments from all those who pass by my corner property.

The law of sowing and reaping has everything to do with the dirt. You have to plant the seed in the good soil to get the return of the seed as it grows into its identity. I love the scripture (Matt 13:3) where Jesus tells the parable about a sower who went out to sow some seed. The story tells the reader about the different places the sower sowed the seed. First he dropped some by the road, where the birds ate the seed up. Other seed fell upon the rocky places, where there was not much soil; the plants sprang up but soon were scorched by the sun because they had no root. Other seed fell among the thorns; the seed again shot up, but up the thorns came and choked them out. Yet other seed fell among good soil and yielded a crop, some a hundredfold, some sixty and some thirty.

This parable may not mean much to you at the moment, but in the coming days and months it will be a necessary component of your recovery. Let's first start with your heart. What does it look like at the moment? Is your heart as hard as the road described in the story, or is it full of thorns, or is it a very rocky place? If you are going to get better and receive help from others and from God Himself, you are going to have to do some tilling in your heart to soften it up to receive truths from God and others so you can get better. I know that what happened to you might not be fair or just, but let's leave that in your past and move on. Your hard heart may have served you well in the past few months as you survived your divorce, but now it's time to pack up shop and move on. God wants to do something new in your life, and your heart needs to be receptive to those new directions and dreams. Don't miss the great things God has just beyond the horizon for you and your children. Staying bitter and mad accomplishes nothing but to keep you stuck in your own past and feelings. Push through the past haunts and till the soil of your heart, soften it up and receive forgiveness and grace and let God restore you and your future.

When you truly get your own soil/heart soft enough to receive seed again, then you can sow into your children and those around you. Then your face will begin to shine and your countenance will let others approach you and sow into you. Good soil is no accident: you have to do your due diligence to keep it free from the weeds and thorns and surround yourself with people who will celebrate you and not drag you back into an attitude of being a victim. It's time to check your pride at the door, take a hard look at your heart and start preparing your soil for the seed that God wants to plant in you. Remember that dirt is what brings seeds to life.

Discover

You may feel really broken at the moment, or maybe just broke. The word *broke* can mean that you have been taken to the cleaners financially by your ex-spouse, but that is not what I want to address on this page. The broke that I am talking about was in the first sentence I just wrote, that you may feel broken by your divorce. A divorce can really cause the wheels to come off from everything you thought you had nailed down in your life. You may not be able to feel anything at the present moment. I can relate to that numb feeling, walking around just devastated by what you have been through. Emotionless is how you feel, just a blank stare coming from your face. You are walking around in a state of shock. You are broke: you don't know what to do, what to say or where to go for help. We gotta get you fixed here on this page and get you moving again.

Turn to 1 Corinthians, chapter 13, and let's start at verse 4:

> *Love is patient, love is kind, and is not jealous; love does not brag and is not arrogant, does not act*

unbecomingly; it does not seek its own, is not provoked, does not take into account a wrong suffered, does not rejoice in unrighteousness, but rejoices with the truth; bears all things, believes all things, hopes all things, endures all things. Love never fails.

Now that is a lot to swallow after what you have been through, but I can tell you from experience that if you will memorize these verses and let them get deep down inside of your heart, you will begin to change. These verses deal with wrongs done to you, and help you not lash out toward others who may have caused you much pain and hurt. These verses appeal to your inner core and ask you to connect to the love that God has to offer you through His son, Jesus Christ.

This kind of love may seem impossible to attain. You will soon find that it is impossible for you to love this way without Jesus in your life. You can't give what you don't have, and these verses demand a more powerful supply than you can muster. To get that supply, you must ask Jesus to come into your heart, after you accept that He has loved you this way by dying on the cross for your sins. With Jesus residing in your heart, you now have a power source that is endless. Jesus is a true example of one who was despised and later put to death on a cross and in His dying breath asked His Heavenly Father to forgive those who put Him to death.

You have been through a lot, but as you look at the life of Jesus, you can see that your circumstances pale compared with what He went through. With Him now in your life you can draw on His power to help you to love again, to learn to forgive. These verses of 1 Corinthians are a blueprint of how to love. Memorize them, ask God to burn them into your spirit, and begin to love others differently. Whatever is holding you back from this transformation, you gotta let it go and discover the riches of loving others with the love that God supplies you every day. Remember, if you're broke, you don't have to stay broke. God's love never fails.

Direction

Many things in this world give us direction. Let's look at a few of these. A map tells us in what direction a certain location is from where we are. A windsock tells the pilots at the airport which direction the wind is blowing so they can fly into the wind on takeoff. A compass is very important to those who are out hunting or working with a map to orient them so they know which direction to go in. The stars in the sky have also directed many a sailor to their ports of call. Many of us feel lost after our divorce, without the routine of our married years. "What do I do now?" or "Where will I go?" are questions you might be asking. I don't know if I can answer those questions specifically for you, but I have some thoughts on the subject of direction for you to ponder.

We all would agree that if we sit and do nothing we will get or go nowhere. Speaking of going nowhere, did you know that it's really impossible for a huge jet to fly? It's too heavy, especially when it's loaded with fuel and passengers. So what is the physics that enables the jet to soar in the sky and do so for hours on end? It's gravity that keeps you and me from floating into space, and that is what keeps the airplane on the ground. So what happens that allows the plane to defy the laws of gravity to suddenly leave the ground and begin to fly? It's the forward motion of the airplane rumbling down the runway that holds the secret. As the plane reaches the right speed the law of gravity gives way to the law of lift. The law of lift now controls the plane and the law of gravity has to take a back seat. As long as the engines supply thrust and keep the plane moving forward, the air rushing over the wings provides the lift necessary to keep the plane in the air. When it's time to land, the pilot just decreases the power and slows the airspeed and the plane begins to feel the tug of gravity. As the plane approaches the runway, the speed diminishes to the point that the law of lift gives the plane back to the earth and gravity now controls it.

Now let's apply that to you. You gotta start moving again in a direction that is peaceful and healing to your soul. With some good counseling in conjunction with setting your priorities in order, you are now ready to start rumbling down the runway of life again. Your speed down the runway will determine when you will be able to fly again. The bigger the plane the longer the runway needed for takeoff, so you will have to measure the length of the runway you will need before the law of lift can grab you and thrust you into the sky. You take the good days with the bad and keep yourself moving, gaining speed and trusting God for your new direction and life.

With God as your copilot you can be assured that your destination will be a perfect fit for the new you and the ones who will be on this flight with you. Just as you put your trust in the pilot when you enter the airplane with your boarding pass and take your seat, you now have to trust God as you let Him take the controls and guide you in a new direction. John 10:27 says, "My sheep hear my voice, and I know them, and they follow me." Do you hear His voice today? God has your ticket, with your departure date, time, and destination. He is waiting for you to board. Trust me; this is a flight you don't want to miss!

Here is a blank page for you to capture those life changing thoughts from the pages you have just read...

Day

Psalms 118 verse 24 says, "This is the day that the Lord has made; Let us rejoice and be glad in it." This life that we lead is made up of days, some more special than others. We all can point to specific days that stand out in our lives, like the birth of children, or our very own birthday. Therefore, we need to look at making the most of our days so we can have as many special days as possible. Every day is to be lived and cherished and treated as a gift from God.

Here are some days that were very special:

1. The day Adam ate the apple
2. The day Noah closed the door on the Ark
3. The day Jesus was born
4. The day Lazarus was raised from the dead
5. The day the blind man received his sight from Jesus
6. The day Jesus was crucified
7. The day He was raised from the dead

8. The day He appeared to the twelve after His resurrection
9. The day Paul was stopped on the road to Damascus by Jesus

As you can see, there are certain days we all can remember. And those days that are in scripture mean different things to each of us because of our different backgrounds. So what are the important days that mark your life? Or, what days that you have yet to live will go down in your history as great days...?

1. The day you were born
2. The day you graduated from high school or college
3. The day you met your spouse
4. The day you were married
5. The day each of your children was born
6. The day you filed for divorce
7. The day your divorce became final...

34. The day you will die

Now you fill in the gap. What are the days that lie out in front of you yet to be lived? Are you excited about your future and the possibilities? If the abovementioned scripture is believed, then you must grasp the truth of what it says. Each day was created by the Lord just for you, the good days and the bad ones alike. The key is to walk through each of them with God, allowing Him to guide you and show you His grace for every day and trial. Remember that moments turn into days and days linked together make up our life that will soon be spent. Let's do better, reach higher and expect more with the days that we have remaining. In the words of my favorite movie character, Forrest Gump, "Have a nice day."

Daughters

Divorce is one of the hardest things I have ever gone through. It's not a journey that has an end; it usually rears its ugly head daily, monthly, and at your most vulnerable moments. Once you figure out that divorce is the gift that keeps on giving the whole year, you can learn how to deal with it.

I have seen athletic teams that start a game with a great strategy of aggressive play, only to change course after building a lead. Now, they choose to play defense; instead of playing to win, they sit on the lead and try not to lose. If you are a sports fan, you know how that usually goes: The other team senses the change of strategy and the tide of the battle beings to turn. As the once aggressive team turns into mush, content to just hang on until the end, the other team begins to gain the momentum. The outcome now is in jeopardy as the change in strategy becomes the key to the final outcome.

I'm now in my eighth year of being a single dad, and the story of my parenting strategy is the reverse of that once aggressive team I described above. After my divorce I was lucky just to be in the parenting game. I spent most of my time on the sidelines, not wanting to play. I was destroyed mentally; I was separated from my children and I thought I had lost them. How was I going to parent them from across town? They were living in a house without me in it, and I was not cool with that. I couldn't change my circumstances, but I had to change my parenting strategy. Not playing is not an option for us dads, especially with our daughters. Proverbs 31 verse 30: "Charm is deceitful and beauty is vain, but a woman who fears the Lord, she shall be praised." As I write these pages my daughters are fourteen and twenty and they are becoming young women very quickly. God has given me wisdom over the past years, and I have sought His strength and the counsel of my pastor and others to grow stronger. I am now off the bench and on the offensive with my daughters, as this window of influence is closing as they grow up.

With God's help I needed to imbed that verse from Proverbs into their spirit. My daughters, all our daughters, need to know that their beauty is from God; He created them, as it says in Psalm 139, and they are fearfully and wonderfully made. No cover of a magazine is going to tell them that truth, and surely some of their friends will be sucked up in the drama of popularity. Every day I can, I tell my daughters how beautiful they are, even if it's on a phone call to my older daughter's college campus. I have to be one of the strongest voices of reason in their minds. I and the Holy Spirit have to be singing a chorus of praise in them as they move through their lives.

Let me now address the second part of that verse, the fearing-God part. How will they learn that if I don't fear God? To truly connect with my daughters, I had to do the connecting through the language of God. Love and forgiveness, grace, acceptance, and just knowing that God is in control and has a wonderful plan for their lives is a message that I needed to model and a language I needed to learn to speak.

This game of life after divorce with your daughters is a game that you can't lose. You must engage them, right every wrong you can, ask for another chance if need be. You are preparing another man's wife here; wouldn't you want a positive stake in her future and the future of your son-in-law one day? Defense is not a winning strategy with daughters.

DAD

EVERY ONE OF US MEN had a dad, but some of us may have never met him or had him around enough to make a difference in our lives. The emotions surrounding this issue are as vast as the sand on the seashore. Feelings of not being wanted by our dad or of being a burden to him are hard memories to erase or get past. The problem is that we take those memories into our marriage and our role as father to our very own children. We can't help but do and say what was done and said to us, both the good and the bad.

Psalms and Proverbs are filled with references to our children being gifts of God to us. They are given to us directly from God, so it's no mistake who your children are—or who your father was, for that matter. My question to you is, how have you handled your gifts? Think about past Christmases or birthdays; what gifts do you remember? Did someone surprise you with exactly what you wanted when you hadn't told a soul what that was? Has a gift just left you speechless, not knowing how to respond? Or have you glibly acted surprised and then afterward discarded the gift in a drawer or closet never to be seen, used or worn in public.

Like it or not, your dad gave you life. Now my question is, what are you doing with that gift? If you are a dad, what are you doing with the gift or gifts that God has given you to raise? I don't have enough space to address every issue, but here goes. If you are a divorced dad, whatever your custody arrangements are, you need to parent those children like there is no tomorrow. My three children were eight, fourteen, and eighteen when they started living mostly with their mother and not with me. We had joint custody, but my job kept me from having them much during the week, so I saw them basically on weekends. I tried not to get bitter, I tried to parent better. I texted, I called—I did everything I could to communicate with them as much as possible. I sacrificed my own personal desires every weekend to do exactly what my children wanted to do. As they got older and became more mobile, I could see them more and they began to have a say in where and who they wanted to be with.

So hang in there. The older your children get the better it will be for you if you are being a positive and trusted parent. I gave 110 percent for my children then and continue to do so even today. When they see your sacrifice it's easy for them to choose you when it's time to discuss the matters of the heart when they get older. Life-changing conversations and life choices will matter later, if you matter now.

Being a great dad is not about you, it's about your children. You have to know them, for them to ever know you. Sow daily and weekly into their lives and trust God that the fruit will be there in His time. The fruit is a God thing, the sowing and giving is a dad thing, so get busy loving your children and listening to them. Care for them. Let them see you as a giver—whatever you have is theirs. The greatest blessing when it comes to your children is that you get to be their dad. God assigned them to you, and if you let that get deep down inside of you will do just fine. Boundaries and structure along with a loving embrace is always a winning combination.

DAISY

SHE LOVES ME, SHE LOVES me not, she loves me, and she loves me not. How many of you have pulled a daisy from a vase or a flower bed and started pulling petals to later see what your answer would be? Answer is, all of us have done this at one time or another, and for the most part its harmless play, but you would be surprised at the number of lives that are lived by making life choices according to this rhyme.

Plucking petals is no way to determine if someone loves you or not, nor is it a good way of making tough choices. Yet we all know folks who go through life making random choices that wreck their lives and the lives of those around them as well. Maybe the reason you are reading my book is that you have been that person making reckless decisions, or you have been showered by the circumstances of once being married to someone who was out of control. Some characteristics of this Russian roulette lifestyle are making decisions on impulse or in secret. Hiding receipts, credit card statements and purchases is no way to build trust in a relationship. Uncontrollable urges to have things that only temporarily bring satisfaction do little to fill the void of poor self-esteem.

Now that you're alone and recovering from your divorce, let's set our compass in a new direction. A direction of purpose that will allow for you to build trust with others and self-esteem back into you. For whatever reason you find yourself on this side of a divorce, you need to know that your life has value. You were created by Almighty God, and it says that you were created in His image. Psalm 139 says that you are "fearfully and wonderfully made," and with that foundation you can now take the randomness out of who you are and out of your choices. Your worth to God will provide purpose to everything you do and where you now go. As you contemplate your new direction based on your God-given destiny, you can now replace the impulse with a carefully thought-out plan. The secrecy you may have experienced can now be lifted as the light of God's word can show you a new path that will help you build trust among your new friends.

Your new life now will look less and less like the one you just left. The key to rising higher is your ability to restructure your thoughts and live to be who God now is calling you to be. With a trusted counselor you can map out a plan and build accountability that will ensure your chances of succeeding. So be encouraged about the newfound freedom that is now at your fingertips and start making better choices today. Use your noggin and think and plan out what you will do and want to accomplish in the days ahead. Let me save you the temptation of repeating the rhyme at the top of this section the next time you spot a vase of daisies… just remember: HE LOVES YOU!

Dynamite

Webster calls dynamite a powerful explosive and we know that it is used to bring down buildings that are ready to be destroyed. Leveling a building this way may seem destructive to the onlooker, but to the contractor, it's necessary because he or she has seen the blueprints of what is to be built in the old building's place. After your divorce, you may feel like an imploded building and perhaps may even look the part. I don't want you to focus on the destruction that you have experienced; rather, turn your attention to the new building/new life that will take its place.

If you have already read the word "Dig," you know the most important part of the new building is the digging of the foundation. How high you want to build depends on how far down you dig the foundation to support the new structure. But with dynamite I want you to focus on the powerful person you still can become. Your marriage may be over, but your new life must go on and it must have hope to be as good as the best parts of your past, or if you're courageous, you can dare to dream for better. I love the encouragement of the Apostle Paul as he was writing Ephesians and closing out chapter 3 in verse 20. Listen to this verse and be inspired: "Now to Him who is able to do exceeding abundantly beyond all that we ask or think, according to the power that works within us."

If you are a believer and have confessed Christ as your savior, this verse is for you. It is full of possibilities for those of us who love the Savior. Knowing that God is able to accomplish beyond our wildest thoughts is just amazing to me. God being able means that He can, and that He alone has the power to pull off anything He wants to do in your life. The link to that power is in the last part of that verse, "according to the power that works within us." It asks us to be linked to God in our spirit and in our heart and mind. Our relationship with Him will bring out His unbelievable plan for our lives. Putting Him on ignore until a crisis overwhelms us is not the relationship that will produce a life full of blessings. Yes, He loves you and you can't escape that, but the relationship that causes His blessings to flow consists of your daily fellowship with Him and including Him in every decision and all that you do. God is not demanding perfection, but what is required is a tender heart and a willingness to give Him your best daily.

So walking with Him will allow you to experience what Paul was talking about. He is able to let you live and experience a life that is beyond all that you could ask or think of. Isn't that incredible! With the mess you may find yourself in at the moment, just know that God stands ready for you to experience a powerful transformation that will blow your mind. Since it's beyond what you can ask or think, you can now focus on being faithful and leave the future to God and His awesome plan for your new life. Just know that your dreams and goals may fall short of what God wants to do, so spend time in prayer with Him and let Him lead you to a life that will amaze others and bless you. Let your new life explode with God's new direction!

Date

The last thing I thought I would be doing at age fifty-three was dating, but my divorce changed all of that and more. I was divorced at age forty-seven, and so many things in my life changed, I had no idea what was around the next corner. Like some of you, I thought I would be married for the length of my or my spouse's life here on earth. When I said "I do," I meant I was in it for life and would stick it out come hell or high water. But sometimes all of your commitment can't stop a marriage from ending.

So there I was, single and wondering, "What now?" That's a feeling that takes some getting used to. Perhaps you had been married for some time and now you find yourself single and at a loss as to what to do or how to act. If you were in your early or mid twenties when you were dating, you knew how to find attractive women to date. It was easy then, but now you're faced with a whole new set of problems. You now have to look for single women in your age bracket, which forces you to look at ring hands to see if they are available. It's a very uneasy place to be and quite scary to do the whole dating thing again. Not to mention that you are being watched by everyone who knows that you're now single, and every one of them is poised to critique every woman you go out with.

The only counsel I can give you is from my experience: give yourself time as you get ready to date. Many times I have mentioned in this book that I had to give myself time to heal from my divorce. I was not going to be any good to anyone if I just rushed into the arms of the first single woman I met. She may have thought that I was cool, but I was in no shape to get involved with her until I had dealt with the damage done by my divorce. I needed to take time to come to terms with what happened to me and then needed more time to let my heart recover and heal before I decided to give it away again. For me, the thought of remaining single sent a feeling of panic racing through my mind; I couldn't handle the thought of growing old alone. All I could think of was that I had just come out of a relationship that ended when it could no longer function. I was tempted to stop using my brain and let my hormones cause me to rush back into the oncoming traffic because of the excuse of not wanting to be alone. I had to start using my head and stop myself from making another mistake. I needed to start trusting the Lord for my singleness just as I would for my salvation.

The Lord is watching and He knows what happened and what you're feeling. It's no mystery to Him as to what will happen; just allow Him to direct your paths as it says in Psalm 119 verse 105. If it's in His will for you to marry again, than start trusting Him for that. Instead of looking for the right person, try becoming the right person so that special someone can be blessed because you took the time to mature yourself during your single days. You need to invest in yourself if you want a better outcome this time around. And when you least expect it, God will cause your paths to cross and then you can ask for that first date.

Distracted

In the Gospel of Luke, chapter 10, you find the story of Martha and her sister Mary. Jesus was in the house for a visit and a meal. Let's pick up the story in verse 39:

> *And she, Martha, had a sister called Mary who moreover was listening to the Lord's word, seated at His feet. But Martha was distracted with all of her preparations; and she came up to Him, and said, "Lord, do You not care that my sister has left me to do all the serving alone? Then tell her to help me." But the Lord answered and said to her, "Martha, Martha, you are worried and bothered about so many things; but only a few things are necessary, really only one, for Mary has chosen the good part, which shall not be taken away from her."*

As you go through your divorce you might say that you're a bit distracted. You are in foreign waters and they are deep and infested with sharks. Your emotions are on edge and your bank account and patience are dwindling. The routine you once knew and enjoyed is a distant memory, and now you are faced with life-changing decisions that you don't want to make. Your focus at work is at risk of going on autopilot. You can't concentrate on one thought for very long. This is not how you are used to living or conducting your life, job or your affairs. If you are not careful, all this unsettledness will cause you to lose your focus and feel like your feet are firmly planted in midair. Another item to contend with is the chatter of all your friends telling you what you should do. They all mean well, but unless they have gone through a divorce themselves, they don't know the half of what you're dealing with. So with all the noise it's easy to become distracted and not pay attention to the most important matters at hand.

If you are distracted at the moment, I would encourage you to get a little selfish with your time and your space. You need some alone time, just like Mary in the scripture above. Get some time alone at the feet of Jesus; that is where the noise will go away and you can then hear the counsel of the Savior. Read the scripture and rediscover how much He loves you and forgives you and wants to help you find your way. The Lord hasn't taken a nap during your trials. He has seen every wrong done to you, and even those times when you haven't acted in the most appropriate way. So He knows it all, and through all the mess His loving arms are extended to you for your benefit. You need to slow down and take the time to hear Him speaking to you in that still, small voice.

Jesus says that Mary had chosen the good part, time spent at His feet and in His presence. Once you figure out that you can't control the actions of others or prevent future calamity, you can hand God all of your fears and let Him fight your battles for you. Give Him all of it, all the things, issues and actions of others that cause you concern. Focus on your peace of mind and what really matters and leave the drama to those who thrive on hysteria. Peace is a place where you completely trust God to work it all out and accept His will for your life. You can't drive and read a road map at the same time; maybe now it's time to pull over and focus on where you are going. Remember, if you don't know where you're going, any road will take you there.

Doctor

I just came from the hospital where my mom underwent hip replacement surgery today, and I want to relate to you an interesting conversation with her surgeon. I was in the pre-op room with my mom, our pastor and my son. We were making small talk and could tell that the time for her surgery was soon to arrive. We bowed in prayer and our pastor prayed for the surgeon and the staff, that they would be guided by the Lord while with my mother in the operating room. Just as we said amen, in walked the surgeon and my mom said, "Just want you to know that we prayed for you to take good care of me." He looked surprised and with eyebrows raised muttered, "Thank you," and then began to ask my mom a series of questions. I kissed my mom and left to go to the waiting room to get some work done on my laptop while the three-hour surgery was beginning. As I sat there I couldn't shake the expression of the surgeon as my mom spoke those words to him.

How many times since your divorce have people told you that they're praying for you? For some of you it has been a long time since you were with folks who are concerned about you. When was the last time someone reached out to you and told you that they were praying for you? I do suppose that you might be reading this page and saying to yourself that not a soul has uttered those kind words to you. In the book of James, chapter 5 verse 16, it says, "The effective prayer of a righteous man can accomplish much." I truly believe that prayer is a great ointment that can cause pain and suffering to be turned around and start the healing process in you.

Maybe you just read that verse and now you're saying, "But I'm not a righteous person, so what am I to do?" Pray! God is a good and caring God and will hear your prayer as you reach out to Him. He is interested in a relationship with you and in your asking Him into your heart and confessing that you're a sinner in need of a savior. That is the first step in getting to know God and accepting all of the forgiveness He wants to extend to you. You can now dump all the guilt and things that have been haunting you from your past mistakes. Give them to the Lord, let Him take your mess and make something beautiful out of your circumstances. The power to live the Christian life lies in the understanding that God Himself wants to live in and through you and give you a place to lay down all the stuff that is keeping you grinding on the past. He died on a cross for all those sins, and He stands ready to help you go forward in a new direction with Him in your life.

You never know who has prayed for you or who is at this very moment praying for you. Get on your knees today and confess that you don't know it all, and that you need Him to help you sort it all out. He knows where you are and all that you're facing today with your children and your now fragmented family. God is the best doctor around. He even makes house calls. He has the power to heal and mend broken lives, so give Him a chance. The doctor will see you now!

Dog

I am in the foodservice business, and in this business the customers we serve happen to be restaurants. No doubt you have eaten at many restaurants in your lifetime and by now you have some favorite haunts that you frequent. For most of you, whatever you are hungry for, you know right where to go for that entrée, and you may even have it dialed down to your favorite booth and server.

For every restaurateur, the menu is what brings you in and drives their profits. Open any menu and you will begin to see what this café does best and what they have to offer. In fact, if you were to walk back into the kitchen you would see that the cooking equipment really drives the menu. You can't prepare and serve what you can't cook, meaning that if you don't have a fryer you can't offer fried foods. Very few restaurants other than buffets will offer everything under the sun; most places just don't have the staff and room in the kitchen to produce all those entrées. As we work with restaurant owners we always start with the menu as it holds the keys to their success. We ask questions like, "When was the last time you changed the items on the menu?" and "When was the last time you raised your prices to reflect the rising cost of the food you buy?" We also ask if the items on the menu are placed correctly in the layout to drive customers to the most profitable items, and if there are too many items on the menu, causing confusion to the patrons.

My first suggestion to the restaurateur is to identify the dogs—the items that aren't selling—and get them off the menu. They are just taking up space on the menu, tying up inventory and precious cash but not making the business any money. It's usually fear that keeps the owner from making such an aggressive change, fear that the one or two customers who order that entrée will object and not come back. What the owner doesn't realize is that another, newer menu idea may attract new customers who will in turn pull many more customers into the restaurant.

I am giving you the same suggestion I give my customers: Get the dogs out of your life and out of your routine. Quit doing and giving energy to the things that neither help you nor interest you. Your divorce has changed things, and you need to change and reorganize your offerings to those around you. What do you like and do best? What makes you happy and falls in line with the gifts that God has given you? It's time that you pursue those things. There may be those who leave your circle due to your changes, and that is fine; your due diligence in changing your personal menu will attract new friends to take their place.

Hebrews 12:1-2: "Let us throw off everything that hinders us and the sin that so easily entangles. And let us run with preference the race marked out for us, fixing our eyes on Jesus the author and perfecter of our faith." Let's replace the dogs in your life with things that won't come back around to bite you.

Dose

While I was living at home with my young family I always became nervous when they got sick. Whatever the illness, we had medication from the doctor or from the drug store that we needed to give them to aid in their recovery. I was always very careful to read the label and make sure I was giving the correct dose. The dose was always given on the side of the bottle or pill container, stating how much and how often the medication was to be administered.

As I began my journey through divorce, this word became very important to me. We are pulled in all directions during those days and experience the widest range of emotions possible. The key for you is to stay as in control of your emotions and responses as possible. As you proceed from the courtroom to a bedroom you have never slept in before, you will have many chances to lose your cool and lash out. While I don't know your situation and every situation is different, you need to have some trusted friends who will hang close during these days. You get to choose the dose of what you tell and when and to whom. You hold the keys to your feelings and to what flows out of your mouth. You need to guard both with the utmost care and remember that everyone around you is not for you.

You are in charge of so much at this point in your life. Your response in this divorce will say a great deal about you. It's so tough at first with the hard realization that you're not married anymore and you may be separated from your children. Your finances may be affected, not to mention those items you bought and paid for, only to have them end up in another man's house. Just remember that you have things that no court can take from you, those being your faith, your joy and the peace that God can bring into your heart. God can settle your tumultuous heart from fearing the unknown; put your faith in Him to handle all the details of how this will all turn out. God is in control and is waiting for you to give the reins to Him and trust that He will guide you in the tough decisions that lie ahead. Read in the book of Exodus of the miracles God provided when the children of Israel left Egypt for the Promised Land. When they were hungry He fed them manna from heaven, and when they were thirsty He brought forth water from a rock. Now, if He can do that, surely He can provide for you during your hour of need.

Increase the dose you receive from God today. Increase the regimen from once in a while to three times a day and see if you don't start to feel better. God is referred to in the scripture as the Great Physician, so let Him do what He is known for: healing hearts and lives. As time starts to pass, you will gain a greater perspective on the situation you find yourself in. With that greater understanding, begin to take positive steps and move your actions and attitude toward becoming that new person God is ready to help you to create. As any doctor will tell you, take all the medicine that is prescribed to you. In God's case His prescription will never need a refill, no matter the dose you're taking into your soul.

Doubt

Now there is a word that will slow the pace and confidence of your life. Doubt is like a cloud that won't give way to the sun. The sun is always shining brightly just beyond the clouds, but when cloud cover is your constant companion you can forget the sun even exists. You become so used to the gloom that your short-term memory takes over and perspective and intelligence go out the window.

The opposite of doubt is confidence. Doubt can paralyze you at any stage in your divorce. On the front end of your divorce the doubt causes you to slow your reactions to the swirling changes that are ending your marriage. Whether you are the one filing or you're being filed against, it makes no matter. Doubt makes second-guessers of us all. The question "Will he or she regain their mind in time to stop this destructive path?" creates doubt. Even with all the documentation that says you should leave...you still are slow to act because of doubt. Am I right? Doubt is a killer and yet it is ever present when we walk down this path we never thought we would tread.

Confidence is a t-shirt that says, "Been there and done that," but confidence is also a distant friend during a divorce. With your heart breaking into pieces and your world now upside down and spinning out of control, you may be looking around for a big red "stop" button you can push to slow the pace and stop the heartache, but there isn't one. Doubt comes along with your hurt and lack of control, and you need to recognize it and learn to deal with it. The sad fact is that when you are going through your divorce your so-called friends scatter. They don't know what to do or say to you, and that puts you further into isolation. The key now is to search for the true friend or pastor who can be your true north and steady your shaky footing. Your divorce may be your first, but God has seen this before and now if you will allow, He will begin to bring to bear all the resources that will carry you through this difficult time.

On the backside of your divorce is the doubt of whether you did the right thing by filing for divorce. Or if it was your spouse who filed, did you do everything to prevent the divorce? Doubt accompanied with regret—this deadly cocktail is one that you don't need to drink or sip. Doubt is as reoccurring as a sunrise on both sides of your divorce. And you need to learn to turn the doubt into a positive energy and recover from its clutches. I have seen many a divorce, including your author's, just paralyze its victims and leave them almost lifeless and wondering if they will ever regain the confidence they used to know.

As I have said repeatedly in this book, nothing is ever the same after divorce. You are a different person after divorce. Your newfound confidence will come from the Savior who will create in you a spirit of renewal and set your life in a new direction with a roadmap of personal restoration and a new life direction to boot. God is a God of second chances and tweaking mistakes into comebacks. If you doubt that, you need to spend some time with Him. Just look at all the characters of the scripture that failed and yet, because of grace, rebounded into a destiny of a changed life.

Here is a blank page for you to capture those life changing thoughts from the pages you have just read...

DRAGON

IN THE BEST OF OLD storytelling it's the fire-breathing dragon that guards the tower to keep the princess from being rescued. The prisoner in the tower is forever captive until the dragon is slain by the rescuer—and you may be surprised by who the rescuer really is or could be and who the prisoner is.

The prisoner may be you and you may find yourself trapped in your own tower. This divorce has isolated you from your friends and your children and you feel trapped with no way out. You may have let others isolate you or you may have isolated yourself... either way, the tower is no place to live in for any length of time. Depending on how long you have been up in the tower, you may have been duped into thinking this is a normal existence and it's all you want or can handle. Your focus on your problems and circumstances has confined you to a room that has no escape because of the past that haunts you, convincing you to hide and make yourself its prisoner. Residing with you in that prison room are fear, hurt, shame and all sorts of thoughts that are misguided and untrue, yet believed by you. For some of you the dragon doesn't have to work very hard to keep you confined, as you are now so jaded that you have accepted this way of life.

May I remind you that if this description fits you, you may need a dose of reality and a bucket of cold water down your back to wake you up? All you have to do to slay that dragon holding you hostage is to walk out of that door, accept what has happened to you and decide to move on with life. There is no lock on that door, and there never has been. In just a short time, you and your professional counselor can have you out of that room and down the staircase and out the castle doors. Remember, as I have said repeatedly, you can't do this alone and expect to be set free. Your mind has to stop the movie of the past and all the circumstances of what happened. You have watched that movie for the last time. Time to choose a new movie, one that will have you playing the role of the rescuer. In that movie, you are the one who will eventually rescue yourself, with God's help. You need to be the answer to your own prayers and seek help and plot a path out of the isolated tower where you have been wasting away.

Seldom will a knight in shining armor and riding a white horse have anything to do with our escape—that is only in fairy tales. Instead, your escape will have much to do with your own desire to break the curse of the past and chart a new course to a new future because you have discovered the new you. You will never be the same person who went through the divorce, so quit taking that person down this new road. The old you doesn't get to go on the new path; only the new you will be able to take the risk and display the courage needed for the new journey. This isn't *Harry Potter*, this is real life. Step out of the captive place and tell the dragon that he is done holding you back. One step at a time with good counsel will always prevail.

DRAMA

There is a reason they call soap operas "daytime drama." The reason these shows are so addicting is that the actions of all the players are continually pushing the limit of accepted behavior. As the drama pushers continue to push, someone else is always on the receiving end of all their antics. The viewers love the back-and-forth, and just when you think the drama couldn't reach another level, some pusher does the unthinkable, and you have to wait until tomorrow to see the fallout of what they did and who was affected. One sure way to stop the drama is to stop watching it and stop reacting to those who push it.

In the book of Luke, chapter 10 verses 38-42, we have the story of Martha and Mary. This is my second reference to this scripture (the first was in "Distracted"). From the story of the sisters we can draw just one more truth to help you with your divorce. We again pick up the story of the sisters as they are entertaining Jesus when He comes to their house for a meal. While the meal preparations are underway, Mary chooses to sit at the feet of Jesus and listen to Him teach. The scripture says that Martha is very distracted with her preparations and she comes up to Jesus and begins to let Him know that Mary is not helping her and that He should do something about the situation. In fact she ends her rant by asking Jesus, "Tell Mary to help me!" After Martha finishes with her drama, Jesus tells her very tenderly, "Martha, Martha, you are upset and worried about many things, but few things are needed, really only one. Mary has chosen what is better."

No doubt the meal preparation was important, as the house was full of guests, but as Martha was ramping up the drama, Jesus stopped it by not reacting to her sales pitch. In effect, Jesus called Martha out and dealt with her head-on, stating that it wasn't about Mary at all, it was about her own poor choice. In effect He was telling Martha that she, not Mary, had it all wrong, that the hustle and bustle of preparing the meal was not to be put before the presence of the Lord.

As you deal with drama in your divorce, you can use this story to understand how to recognize it and deal with it. Usually it's those who are caught up in the drama and produce the hysteria that have it all wrong. They are far more interested in pushing their agenda than in the truth of the matter. If what they believed was so right, they wouldn't need the drama to make it so convincing, they could just let the facts speak for themselves. The *truth* never needs drama to make its argument in a conversation, nor does it need the assistance of anyone to make its case. Truth can stand on its own two feet, and no amount of drama can change its effect on a matter.

Always seek the truth and stand on the side of truth in any discussion or decision. Let the other side rant and rally others to their position all they want; in the end the truth will prevail and whatever untruths they held to so tightly will be exposed. Don't get caught up in it and succumb to the pressure that drama pushers apply to get you to consent to their wishes. Remember, it's almost always about them and what they want, no matter the consequences that may befall you or your children. Stop the drama with the truth and with a calm response. Your objective is to stop drama in its tracks before you find yourself run over by it.

Dream

All of us have our own opinions about dreams. And depending on your state of mind as you read this page, you may or may not be ready to hang with me for the next five minutes. For those who want to indulge their minds about what the future could hold, let's take a few stabs at what is in your heart.

Psalm 37 verses 1-7 talks about God's willingness to give you the desires of your heart, or dreams if you will. Since you are His creation, it is He who put the desires there for you to discover. The trouble with our desires and dreams is they get buried underneath years of caring for others, raising children and working at our jobs. We only really think about our dreams as we scratch a lotto ticket and imagine what we would do if we won the Powerball.

Why is it that these may be the only times we think about our dreams? Are your dreams tied to money? I really think that the reason we have stopped dreaming is because we think our dreams are too lofty. We never really spend any time thinking about how we are going to get there. Dreams of living our lives in a hut on a beach somewhere in the tropics aren't very productive and will bless you but no one else. Our lives are meant to be lived, and from our blessings we are to bless other people. I think that we need to scale down our dreams following our divorces and set our dream level to dreams of peace in our very own lives. Dreams of getting back in touch with your heart and who you really are now that you are on your own again. Now you have the time to spend alone and search your own heart and see what God put there to bring you happiness.

Your happiness will come from doing the will of God. If you have spent your married life trying to make your spouse happy and never being allowed to focus on what makes you happy, you may feel uneasy about focusing on yourself. It's not selfish to focus on yourself; in fact it's the healthiest thing you can do.

As you spend time alone and ask yourself what your desires are, you may be surprised at what you find. As you now can spend time doing what you like, you will also find yourself with more opportunity to be happy and enjoy your new life and its direction. With your happiness now connected to God and your desires, you can dream some dreams that make sense and are constructive to your direction in life. Now your dreams have a chance of coming true as you have a path and a clear road map of how you can really make that happen. Whether it's more education or a new skill you need, now you can go get that needed addition and take that next step toward your God-given destiny.

As you match your desires with what God put in your heart, you can ask God to give life to those dreams that you feel connected to because of Him. So the once lofty goals are within reach with some hard work and effort. As you make those tiny steps toward your desires, you will gain momentum with every victory and put yourself one step closer to that dream. Dreams are not only for those who sleep but for those who have something to live for.

DRINK

WHAT IS YOUR FAVORITE BEVERAGE? I know, it really depends on what you're doing or what you're eating, right? If you're sitting with a stack of Oreo cookies, then the only answer is a tall glass of cold milk to chase those bad boys. If, on the other hand, it's your favorite cut of meat cooked just the way you like it, then perhaps a glass of wine will complement the protein. In fact going through a divorce can cause you to rethink *what* goes with *what* in your new life. Now that you have been stripped of your married life and are embarking on a new venture, it's worth the discussion of how to begin again and how to embrace this fresh start.

Jesus is speaking in Matthew 9:17, and says, "Nor do men put new wine into old wineskins; otherwise the wineskins burst, and the wine pours out, and the wineskins are ruined; but they put new wine into fresh wineskins, and both are preserved." The message from Jesus was that the tired old religion of the Pharisees was corrupt and was not to be tied to the Good News that He was preaching. Jesus' message was not to be in any way associated with what the Pharisees were teaching; they were different and needed to be treated that way. The use of wineskins in the illustration was to show that the old rigid wineskins could not hold new wine, because the new wine would cause them to burst. The new wine demanded new wineskins, so as the new wine fermented and expanded, the new skins could expand with it and would not split or crack.

Now let's apply this to you. Now that you're divorced, you cannot stuff your new life into your old way of thinking. God wants to do something new and exciting in your life, and pouring your new life into those old wineskins of your past thoughts and prejudices will not work. You need to leave those thoughts and beliefs behind and let God pour out your new life into a new wineskin. Your past marriage has taken its toll on you, and staying with that mentality will only cause you to stay stuck in a rut. Living in the past and finding new folks to tell your story of woe is not, in my book, moving on. Moving on means first asking God to forgive you for your part in the mess, then learning to forgive others, and lastly, starting to forget. Savoring any lingering bitterness will only taint your desire to move on and be happy. Let it go, and fix your eyes on the man God wants to now make you into. When you become a new wineskin, God will then start to pour the new wine into you. As He begins to pour, you will be stretched and challenged to hold more and more of what God wants to pour into you. As you stretch, it may not be comfortable at first, but as you realize who is doing the filling, you will enjoy every drop of new wine.

Spend some time with this scripture and let it sink into your heart. You don't have another three to seven years to waste by repeating the same mistakes again. Your new thoughts need to be accompanied by a new life, and the scripture paints a perfect picture of that for you. You don't want this new life to be spilled out by pouring it into a container that has seen better days. New wine, new wineskin—that is the new *what* goes with *what*.

PRND321

Recognize this series of characters? This is what you see when you get into your car as you fire it up and get ready to *drive*. We have all known what the symbols stand for ever since the first time we sat behind the wheel…well, let's at least hope you know what they all mean by now!

These symbols are a good reminder for you as you live out your divorce. Let's spend some time creating some healthy reminders that you can think of the next time you crawl behind the wheel. Our lives, if you will, have gears just like our cars. I'm sure you can remember times when you felt like you were stuck in park and then times when you felt like you were firmly in drive and couldn't be stopped. No doubt you can even remember times when it felt like you were in reverse and going backward through life. Life sure has its gears, doesn't it?

Time waits for no one. The seconds turn into minutes, and minutes turn into hours…you get the picture. Regardless of what happens in the world or to you, time marches on and carries you with it. You can't control it. Another thing you can't control is the actions and decisions of others, and sometimes those decisions involve you. We get swept up in these tidal waves because of relationships that connect us to others. Whether at work or at home, the actions of others overlap our life and we are affected. That is why you are reading this book: because of either your actions or the actions of your ex-spouse, you have been through or are now going through a divorce. Again it's a process of moving forward until the divorce is final and you walk away a single man.

I know after I moved out, I put myself in the three lower gears, *3 2 1*, to slow my descent. These lower gears slow your car without burning out your brakes. I have a customer located atop Wolf Creek Pass in Colorado. When I finish a sales call there and begin to head back down the mountain, I frequently use the lower gears to slow my SUV. You may feel like you are in a descent after your divorce; that is when your close friends can help break your fall with some gentle conversation and support. In the months that followed my divorce I felt like I was going in reverse, when I realized I had left with only my clothes and my car. I spent eighteen years in a marriage only to have to start from scratch with just some personal belongings. Then there are the times when you feel like you're in neutral, just existing but not covering any real ground. You're not even spinning your wheels; the motor is running but you're not engaged and moving forward.

The goal of any recovery is to get you into drive, moving forward with purpose. Peter in Acts chapter 12 is in prison, chained between two guards. Suddenly an angel of the Lord appeared and the chains fell off of Peter's hands and the angel led him out of the prison. The situation looked hopeless and yet God was watching and acted in his behalf. God knows where you are and what you've been through, so don't lose heart. Trust Him to care for you and come to your rescue in your time of need. The key is for you to allow Him to rescue you, His way and in His timing. With all of your circumstances pressing in on every side, it's easy to get frustrated that your rescue is taking too long. Take heart: the same God that sent an angel to Peter can still send one your way, one day, and His way.

Drown

Few things strike as much fear into the hearts of parents as this word does in the summer months. Swimming pools, outings at the lake, or just teenagers rafting down a ditch unsupervised, are all fun and exciting yet can turn deadly. Water is to be respected and whenever you are near it or in it, you have to be prepared. In the word "Decide," you read about the disciples and Jesus walking on the water. Now I want to again take you to the book of Matthew and pull one more example out of that story.

In Matthew 14:26, we see Jesus walking on the water to come to the disciples. The disciples were in their fishing boat and the scripture says that when they saw Jesus they were frightened, thinking they were seeing a ghost. Verses 27 through 32 tell us what happened next, after Jesus told them not to be afraid, saying, "It is I":

> *And Peter answered Him and said, "Lord, if it is you, command me to come to You on the water." And He said, "Come." And Peter got out of the boat, and*

walked on the water and came toward Jesus. But seeing the wind, he became afraid, and beginning to sink, he cried out, saying, "Lord, save me!" And immediately Jesus stretched out His hand and took hold of him, and said to him, "O you of little faith, why did you doubt?"

Peter had been a fisherman for a long time, and he knew that things that don't belong on the water will sink. Yet when faced with the opportunity to leave the safety of the boat and join Jesus on the water, he went for it. The fact that Jesus said "Come" made all the difference and made the risk worth the reward. Why did the other eleven stay in the boat? Even after seeing Peter get out of the boat and start walking on the water, they all still sat there and did nothing.

May I apply this to your life? Now that you're divorced and moving in a new direction, it's going to be very tempting to stay in the boat where it's safe. In the boat is where you are familiar, it's where your friends are, it's what you have known all your married life. But as He did with Peter, Jesus will call you out of your boat to walk on the sea. He will call you to do something different, something you have never done before, but as you walk on the sea, you will be walking toward Jesus. As you step out of your boat, your friends are going to tell you that you can't do it, it can't be done, and you have no business doing that. At that moment you have to decide who you are going to listen to. Are you going to listen to the boat people in your life who love to criticize everyone else yet never do anything themselves? Or are you going to muster the courage to step out of your boat and walk toward Jesus? What lies on the sea as you walk toward Jesus is the destiny that He has for you. Your new life awaits; it's a life that you have not known. Also know that you can't walk on water with a boat mentality. You have to let go of what others think about you and what you have thought about yourself up to this point. When you step out of the boat, you leave the past behind and step into your new life.

Realize that this is not a onetime event: you need to step out of your boat every day and surround yourself with friends who will allow you and support your stepping out of your boat. You can't be surrounded by boat people and walk very long on the sea. Despite the wind and waves that may frighten you, keep on watching Jesus and not the elements; it's Jesus who is calling you. As Jesus did for Peter when he became afraid and started to sink, His hand will be outstretched in your direction. You won't drown with Jesus walking by your side on the water, but to do that, you must first have the courage to get out of the boat!

Due

If you have ever been a fan of baseball you are familiar with the phrase "He's due!" It's what we commonly utter when a hitter has gone several at bats with no hits. What we mean is, odds are if the batter keeps swinging, soon he will get a hit. There is a connection between hard work and being due that we sometimes forget. Sitting around and watching the grass grow or the paint dry will not increase the odds of your producing anything significant. The hitters I spoke of, although they went hitless in their last few times at bat, are daily spending countless hours in the batting cage working on their form and timing.

In the book of Galatians, chapter 6 verse 9 talks about the law of sowing and reaping. "And let us not lose heart in doing good, for in *due* time we shall reap if we do not grow weary." I am sure I can hear you now groaning at my encouragement to do good when you feel like crap with all that you are going through. You might be saying, "How can I even think about doing good when I am getting the shaft and dealing with attorneys and someone hell-bent on taking me to the cleaners?" I can understand your concerns of fairness and your feeling justified to spew back everything that is coming at you, but really what good does that do you? Jumping into the pit to wrestle with pigs will only get you as dirty as the one you are fighting with.

The key to the scripture I suggested above is preserving your character and not losing your heart for God. At the moment you lose your heart, everything else starts to unravel and you become someone you don't recognize. In your physical body, the heart pumps the needed oxygen-enriched blood to all areas so the body can function properly; you stop the heart and you stop everything. The same principle applies to your spirit/heart: If you allow your spirit to lose its joy and purpose, you cut the lifeline to your ever being a blessing to anyone around you. When you lose heart you stop thinking of others and how you can better those around you. You then turn inward and become selfish and concerned only with you getting yours before anyone else. In the intense battle you may be in right now, my coaching to you is to maintain your heart for God and for those around you. You can still fight for what's right and protect yourself, but do it in a calm and mature manner. Keep trusting that God is going before you in all matters.

If God truly owns it all anyway, you're better off doing it His way, would you not agree? Sow as He instructs us to do and then reap the best that only He can give. God can bless your life a hundredfold more than you could ever do on your own, so quit trying to get yours at the expense of others. Let God deal with those who would do you harm; you be about protecting your heart and start looking for ways to do good to those around you. Your path out of the mess you're in will become clear only with you firmly gripping His strong Hand. Hold on tight, for as you start walking with Him your heart will grow stronger and doing good will become a way of life. Your life of blessing won't be a hit-and-miss affair anymore. Keep sowing and the promise of God is what you will reap. Keep your heart strong in everything you *due*!

Duet

In your music-listening past, who were your favorite duets? Was it Donnie and Marie, Loretta Lynn and Conway Twitty, or maybe some other star duet? You may have liked the song or maybe it was the artists, but some people just sound better together. The definition that Webster gives for *duet* is "a composition for two voices." That is the thought I want to challenge you with for the next few minutes.

Despite the pain associated with a divorce, many are willing to remarry while others have had enough. Divorce takes a toll on your spirit and soul. The rejection, fallout of children, finances… It's enough to really diminish the chances of anyone taking another shot at marriage. Yet the scripture continues to call many of us back to the altar someday.

Genesis 2:18 says, "Then the Lord God said, 'It is not good for man to be alone; I will make a helper suitable for him.'" We are all in a sense created for companionship. Now that is not a command for everyone to be married, but companionship seems to be the theme here. I think the best part of a healthy marriage is the companionship and sense of partnership that the bonds of matrimony bring.

It's no fun to be on your own and alone, yet I found that the time I spent alone after my divorce was the place where I healed and gathered strength to go on. After eighteen years of marriage, time seemed to creep by during the many quiet afternoons, nights and weekends I faced as a single man. At age fifty-three, I just wondered who would want to spend the rest of their life with me. Those doubts used to haunt me as I just thought that I would never find another woman to sleep on the other side of my bed. When I began to put that desire in the hands of God and take seriously the call of my Christian counselor to fix my broken parts and start to see myself as God sees me, then my attitude changed.

I began to see dating as not so much me looking for the right person, but rather me becoming the right person. To go through a major overhaul at midlife was not my choice for how to spend my free time, but it was the correct path for me to one day become attractive enough to lure another woman into a relationship with me. You don't want to go out looking to date another woman when there are parts of you that need fixing. It's not her job to fix you. Instead, you want her to see you as an attractive man who can lead her and her children, if there are any. She needs to see you as able to provide and be faithful to her and to the Lord. If you ever want to sing again with another woman, you need to be able to sing your part. In the same manner you need a woman who can sing in harmony with you, someone who sings on key and knows her part.

If you are to be in a duet again, both partners have to be able to sing together. Each of you must know your own part and when it's your time to sing and your time to be silent. Can you and your partner sing together? Do you have harmony with her, or are you so overbearing you drown out her voice? A duet is an arrangement in which both have to listen to each other as they sing. The definition of duet is just doing anything together, and choosing to do it so well that all you hear is one voice.

Door

Ever lost your keys? That is the most unsettling feeling; you are stuck until you find them. After you slap your pockets and dig in them just one more time, you then begin to turn your house or apartment upside down to find those keys. Okay, where was the last place or time you remember having them? You might search for a minute or an hour, but when you finally find them it's always a relief. Now life is getting back to normal.

A key can either open something or start something. Your key can open the door to your car or truck and once in the ignition it can start the engine. Keys are always tied to ownership, meaning that your keys won't start my car and my key won't open the front door of your house. We all have a set of keys on a ring and each key goes to something or it shouldn't be on the ring. Have you ever had a key that you haven't used? You soon forget what it goes to, and before long it ends up in the bottom of some drawer.

My point in this discussion is that there are keys out there to help you on your post-divorce path. You will soon discover that you have to get moving and start down a path you will walk by yourself.

No longer married, you need to decide to open a few doors and start doing some things that are going to be good for you.

One key I would suggest to you would be to stay single for a while and reconnect with yourself. Be open to not jumping into another relationship; you need time to focus on yourself. Another key is to pay attention. Pay attention to what you like and don't like. Pay attention to the pain and anger that still may reside in your heart. A third key is to practice some forgiveness. Let the bitterness go and let joy be the determining factor of how you face life now. God stands ready with open arms to help you start over and get a vision for the great things that await you. You will never see those things if you are still drowning in regret and woulda, coulda, shoulda.

The next time you pick up your keys to go somewhere or open a door, practice the thought that there is a set of keys in your heart just waiting to be found. In Revelation 3:20 Jesus states that He stands at the door and knocks and "if anyone hears My voice and opens the door, I will come in to him." Your heart has a door; open it today to the Savior.

DEFINE

NO DOUBT AS YOU HAVE pushed your way through this effort of mine, you have been presented with many of my encouragements to survive and recover from your divorce. Some of my ideas you may embrace, and I am sure that we haven't seen eye to eye on some others. That is what any exchange of ideas will bring out, and I truly hope that I have been some help to you. I have one last thought to pass in front of you, and it is this: What will you allow to define your life, this divorce or something else?

In the book of Acts starting in chapter 9 we are introduced to Saul. He was a hater of Christians and a witness at many stoning deaths of the same. No doubt his life was one of death and persecuting those who were followers of Jesus. All that came to a screeching halt one day as he journeyed to Damascus. While on the road he was surrounded by a light from heaven and it flashed all around him. A voice was saying to him, "Saul, Saul, why are you persecuting Me?" The voice was that of Jesus, and with the brightness of the light, Saul was now blind. Jesus, now resurrected, spoke to a man named Ananias, telling him to go find Saul and lay his hands on him. When Ananias did so, Saul received back his sight, and the remaking of Saul began.

You need to read the rest of the story to see that Saul's name was later changed to Paul and he ended up writing most of the New Testament that we have today. As he writes in the book of Ephesians, chapter 1 verse 18, "I pray that the eyes of your heart may be enlightened, so that you may know what is the hope of His calling." Paul, once blinded by the light of the Savior, now relates the understanding of the hope of the calling of God as he recalls his own experience. His eyes were once blinded, but after the encounter with Jesus Paul relates knowing Him with those same eyes that had been blind. How beautiful his encouragement to us that our knowing of the calling of the Savior should come from the eyes of our heart. Once blinded, now they can see and grasp the eternal will of the Creator.

In Paul's past, when he was known as Saul, he was a man who did much harm. But Paul didn't let his past define him. Rather, he let a defining moment change his life forever in a most positive way. We all have things that have happened to us or are happening at this very moment; the key is to allow those experiences to shape us in a positive way like Paul did.

You have a choice concerning this divorce: you can forever blame it for your plight, or you can let it be a defining moment where you embrace the course correction. It's a matter of head position, and you get to choose which direction you turn your head, whether you look back or look forward. Looking back will just enslave you to what happened and that scene will never change. But a forward view will allow you to see all of the new things that God has for you in your future. As Paul says, "May the eyes of your heart be enlightened"—that is a forward statement.

God wants to show you the endless supply of His grace and mercy by showing you more and more of Him. May your new life be defined not by what has happened to you, but rather by whom you have now come to be. Use all of life's lessons to shape you and teach you that God does have a plan, and that He does love you very much. So keep pushing past the hurt of your divorce and allow God to do something new and exciting in you. Allow God to use life's issues to shape you and define you, always looking forward, knowing He is there with you every step of the way.

Congratulations, you have just finished the book and I trust that you have been blessed and helped by its content. On this last page, my hope is that you will jot down some final thoughts that you can refer to as the days pass. Time will do its part in the healing process, but the hard work that lies ahead for you must be done. No short cuts in healing from a Divorce, get into counseling and take your healing that you receive from God and share with those you love in your new life. LB

Made in the USA
San Bernardino, CA
17 May 2014